ICT

INFORMATION AND
COMMUNICATIONS
TECHNOLOGY

FLUENCY AND HIGH SCHOOLS

A WORKSHOP SUMMARY

Steven Marcus, Rapporteur

Planning Committee on ICT Fluency and
High School Graduation Outcomes

Board on Science Education

Center for Education

Division of Behavioral and Social Sciences and Education

NATIONAL RESEARCH COUNCIL
OF THE NATIONAL ACADEMIES

THE NATIONAL ACADEMIES PRESS
Washington, D.C.
www.nap.edu

THE NATIONAL ACADEMIES PRESS 500 Fifth Street, N.W. Washington, DC 20001

NOTICE: The project that is the subject of this report was approved by the Governing Board of the National Research Council, whose members are drawn from the councils of the National Academy of Sciences, the National Academy of Engineering, and the Institute of Medicine. The members of the committee responsible for the report were chosen for their special competences and with regard for appropriate balance.

This study was supported by Grant No. ESI-0102582 between the National Academy of Sciences and the National Science Foundation. Any opinions, findings, conclusions, or recommendations expressed in this publication are those of the author(s) and do not necessarily reflect the views of the organizations or agencies that provided support for the project.

International Standard Book Number 0-309-10246-4

Additional copies of this report are available from the National Academies Press, 500 Fifth Street, N.W., Lockbox 385, Washington, DC 20055; (800) 624-6242 or (202) 334-3313 (in the Washington metropolitan area); Internet, http://www.nap.edu.

Suggested citation: National Research Council. (2006). *ICT Fluency and High Schools: A Workshop Summary.* S. Marcus, Rapporteur. Planning Committee on ICT Fluency and High School Graduation Outcomes. Board on Science Education, Center for Education. Division of Behavioral and Social Sciences and Education. Washington, DC: The National Academies Press.

THE NATIONAL ACADEMIES
Advisers to the Nation on Science, Engineering, and Medicine

The **National Academy of Sciences** is a private, nonprofit, self-perpetuating society of distinguished scholars engaged in scientific and engineering research, dedicated to the furtherance of science and technology and to their use for the general welfare. Upon the authority of the charter granted to it by the Congress in 1863, the Academy has a mandate that requires it to advise the federal government on scientific and technical matters. Dr. Ralph J. Cicerone is president of the National Academy of Sciences.

The **National Academy of Engineering** was established in 1964, under the charter of the National Academy of Sciences, as a parallel organization of outstanding engineers. It is autonomous in its administration and in the selection of its members, sharing with the National Academy of Sciences the responsibility for advising the federal government. The National Academy of Engineering also sponsors engineering programs aimed at meeting national needs, encourages education and research, and recognizes the superior achievements of engineers. Dr. Wm. A. Wulf is president of the National Academy of Engineering.

The **Institute of Medicine** was established in 1970 by the National Academy of Sciences to secure the services of eminent members of appropriate professions in the examination of policy matters pertaining to the health of the public. The Institute acts under the responsibility given to the National Academy of Sciences by its congressional charter to be an adviser to the federal government and, upon its own initiative, to identify issues of medical care, research, and education. Dr. Harvey V. Fineberg is president of the Institute of Medicine.

The **National Research Council** was organized by the National Academy of Sciences in 1916 to associate the broad community of science and technology with the Academy's purposes of furthering knowledge and advising the federal government. Functioning in accordance with general policies determined by the Academy, the Council has become the principal operating agency of both the National Academy of Sciences and the National Academy of Engineering in providing services to the government, the public, and the scientific and engineering communities. The Council is administered jointly by both Academies and the Institute of Medicine. Dr. Ralph J. Cicerone and Dr. Wm. A. Wulf are chair and vice chair, respectively, of the National Research Council.

www.national-academies.org

Acknowledgments

The National Research Council (NRC), through the Center for Education and its Board on Science Education in consultation with the NRC's Computer Science and Technology Board, was asked by the National Science Foundation (NSF) to hold a workshop to explore which components of fluency with information and communications technology can best be developed during the high school years. This report is the outgrowth of that workshop, held in Washington, DC, on October 23–24, 2005. The workshop would not have become a reality without the generous support of the NSF's Advanced Technological Education Program and the encouragement and thoughtful guidance provided by Gerhard Salinger and Michael Haney, program directors in NSF's Elementary, Secondary, and Informal Education Division.

As workshop chair, I wish to extend my thanks to my colleagues who served on the planning committee, each of whom brought deep and varied experiences to the process of planning the workshop. It was a talented and thoughtful group who gave generously of their knowledge and time. I also wish to thank Herb Lin, director of the Computer Science and Technology Board, for his ongoing consultation.

I wish to thank the following individuals who presented at the workshop: Thomas N. Applegate, executive dean, Austin Community College; John Behrens, senior manager, Assessment Development and Innovation, Cisco Systems Inc.; Karen Bruett, director, Education & Community Initiatives, Dell, Inc.; Chris Dede, Timothy E. Wirth professor of learning technologies, Harvard Graduate School of Education; Julia Fallon, program developer for technical education, Office of Superintendent of Public Instruction, WA; Wendy Hawkins, executive director, Intel Foundation; Martin Ripley, head of e-strategy, Qualifications Curriculum Authority, U.K.; Robert Tinker, President, Concord Consortium; and Vera Michalchik, research social scientist, SRI.

Special thanks go to the authors of four papers that helped hone our thinking prior and during the workshop: Philip Bell, associate professor, University of Washington, and liaison from the Board on Science Education; Paul Horwitz, senior scientist, Concord Consortium; Karen Pittman, president, Forum for Youth Investment; and Paul Resta, director, Learning Technology Center, University of Texas.

I would like to thank the staff of the Board on Science Education. The intelligent oversight of director Jean Moon guided our deliberations and helped us to chart an effective course. The entire committee process was aided enormously by the skilled and highly competent work of Heidi Schweingruber, senior program officer. Kemi Yai, senior program assistant for the Board on Science Education, deserves special thanks for attending to the many and varied logistics and technologies the workshop involved.

Finally, I would like to thank Steven Marcus who wrote this report and did a wonderful job capturing the many ideas—large and small—in the workshops.

This report has been reviewed in draft form by individuals chosen for their diverse perspectives and technical expertise, in accordance with procedures approved by the NRC's RRC. The purpose of this independent review is to provide candid and critical comments that will assist the institution in making its published report as sound as possible and to ensure that the report meets institutional standards for objectivity, evidence, and responsiveness to the study charge. The review comments and draft manuscript remain confidential to protect the integrity of the deliberative process. We thank the following individuals for their review of this report: Michael Eisenberg, Information School, University of Washington; Steve Robinson, Albert Einstein Fellow, Office of Senator Barack Obama, Washington, DC; and Nancy Butler Songer, Science Education and Learning Technologies, School of Education, University of Michigan.

Although the reviewers listed above provided many constructive comments and suggestions, they were not asked to endorse the content of the report nor did they see the final draft of the report before its release. Tom Keller, Secondary Instruction, Medomak Valley High School, Waldoboro,

ME, oversaw the review of this report. Appointed by the NRC, he was responsible for making certain that an independent examination of this report was carried out in accordance with institutional procedures and that all review comments were carefully considered. Responsibility for the final content of this report rests entirely with the author and the institution.

Margaret Honey, *Chair*
Planning Committee on ICT Fluency and
High School Graduation Outcomes

Contents

1 Background   1
   Margaret Honey
2 Introduction   6
3 ICT Fluency in the 21st Century   12
4 Perspectives on High Schools   23
5 What Are High School Students Learning? Where and How
   Are They Learning It?   35
6 Assessments to Measure Students' Competencies   45
7 Revisiting the *Being Fluent* Framework   53
8 Afterword   65
   Jean Moon and Heidi Schweingruber

Appendixes
A ICT Fluency: Content and Context   69
   Karen Pittman
B Achieving Information and Communications
   Technology (ICT) Fluency: Is Nothing New Under the Sun?   73
   Paul Horwitz
C Cognitive and Social Foundations of Information and
   Communications Technology (ICT) Fluency   77
   Philip Bell
D Information and Communications Technology (ICT) Fluency:
   What Do All High School Students Need to Know?   86
   Paul Resta

1

Background

Margaret Honey

This report summarizes a workshop held at the National Academies in October 2005 to explore how high schools should respond to calls for increasing fluency with information and communications technology (ICT) among American adolescents. The workshop was designed to extend the work begun in the report *Being Fluent with Information Technology* (National Research Council, 1999), which identified key components of ICT fluency and discussed their implications for undergraduate education. A focus on ICT fluency is particularly timely today, with renewed national attention being paid to global competitiveness of the U.S. workforce, especially in science and technology (NRC, 2006). However, the need for supporting high school students' ICT competencies has been recognized since the 1980s.

In 1983, the federal report *A Nation at Risk* (National Commission on Excellence in Education, 1983) included a recommendation that high school graduation requirements include coverage of the "five new basics"— English, mathematics, science, social studies, and computer science. The report also specified that all high school graduates should "understand the computer as an information, computation and communication device; [be able to] use the computer in the study of the other Basics and for personal and work-related purposes; and understand the world of computers, electronics, and related technologies" (p. 26).

Nearly 20 years later, the No Child Left Behind Act of 2001 included a recommendation that by the eighth grade all students be technologically literate, and it repeatedly referenced technology as an important source of support for teaching and learning across the curriculum. Pushing the bar a bit higher, America's corporate leaders have been saying for some time that technology must not only be used effectively and creatively by students but also be understood in ways that move students beyond basic levels of competency.

In recent years, technology fluency has become a focal point for education ministries worldwide. They and their nongovernmental counterparts have issued white papers, for instance, that connect technological fluency with the critical-reasoning abilities required in the information age (de Ricjke, 2004; Korean Ministry of Education and Human Resources Development, 2003). Educational leaders and policy makers have also responded to the growing importance of technology in the global marketplace, and in classrooms, with programs designed to prepare young people to compete in the international information community.

China, for example, has made information technology part of the compulsory coursework for all of its high school students, who are now expected to be able to collect, analyze, and communicate information (Feicheng and Cuihua, 2002). Singapore, recognizing the vital role that education will play in the country's planned transformation to a center of technological innovation, has established instruction in creativity and innovation as part of its centralized curriculum (Kozma, 2005). Australia has promoted throughout its states and territories ICT in Schools, a program to foster ICT training and use in the classroom (Woods, 2004). South Korea's national curriculum has identified within its top-level goals for high school students their need to prepare for the global setting (Korea Institute of Curriculum and Evaluation, 2005). That nation's underlying technological infrastructure further supports this educational push; South Korea has become a world leader in the number of households with access to broadband Internet connections (Herz, 2002).

In Europe, Finland has created programs to support teachers and students in developing knowledge-building skills through student-centered approaches to teaching and learning linked to communities and local businesses. At the same time, the United Kingdom has drawn considerable attention from its European and Asian counterparts with an innovative assessment, the Key Stage ICT Literacy Assessment for children ages 12–13. Created by the British government's Qualifications and Curriculum Authority, the Key Stage 3 test is designed both to gauge students' ability to apply critical thinking skills—using technology to solve complex problems within a novel testing environment—and to support educators in teaching these skills to their students (Kozma, 2005; Partnership for 21st Century Skills, 2005; Walton, 2005). Ministries in other countries have expressed interest in adapting this assessment and associated strategies to their own school systems[1]

The United States, meanwhile, faces a curricular challenge, despite its early recognition of the need for ICT education. While we attempt to ensure that every American child has a quality education in the traditional basic subjects, other countries have recalibrated their educational institutions to respond differently to the challenge of learning for the 21st century. The argument can be made that if we continue to limit our educational focus to traditional core subjects, our students may lack the skills that are critical to succeeding in the new global marketplace that places technology and communications at the center of work and learning.

The need to change this situation has not gone unattended, however. Seven years ago, the NRC's forward-thinking *Being Fluent with Information Technology* spelled out the three major components—with 10 specific competencies under each component—that comprise what is needed in the ICT domain by young people today (National Research Council, 1999, pp. 2–3):

1. contemporary ICT skills: the ability to use current computer applications;
2. foundational ICT concepts: the basic principles and ideas of computing, networking, and information science; and
3. intellectual capabilities: the ability to apply ICT in complex and sustained situations and to practice higher-level thinking in ICT contexts.

The 1999 NRC report struck a chord with U.S. colleges and universities. It was quickly adopted in course curricula, while college textbooks were modified to explain the components and competencies outlined in the report and expand on them (Snyder, 2006). Yet the report has attracted

---

[1]Personal communications in November 2004: S.C. Leong. Singapore Examinations and Assessment Board, N. Law. Director, Centre for Information Technology in Education, O. Erstad, Head of Research, Network for IT Research and Competence in Education. Norway, and M. Ripley, Head of e-Strategy Qualifications and Curriculum Authority.

modest attention and a more measured response from K–12 educators, particularly from the nation's high schools. At present, the curricula of most U.S. high schools are limited to such current ICT tools or skills as word processing or facility with using Internet search engines. While tool and skill acquisition is important, it is just one component of ICT fluency as defined in *Being Fluent with Information Technology.*

Indeed, the underlying concepts and intellectual capabilities—which can be developed through the application of technology tools to manage and represent complexity, solve problems, and think critically, creatively, and systematically about solutions—remain woefully underdeveloped across the high school years. While educators and policy makers have come to view ICT literacy as a critical part of the requirements for high school graduates, little progress has been made in establishing a trajectory of competencies to guide educators in incorporating ICT into academic content.

The present report extends the work of *Being Fluent with Information Technology* in three ways: (1) examining the need for updates to the 1999 report's ICT fluency framework; (2) identifying the most promising current efforts for developing high school students' ICT competencies; and (3) presenting new information on leading-edge assessment practices that can be used to measure those competencies.

In short, our hope is that this report sheds new light on the kinds of skills and habits of mind that should now be required of students for them to succeed as global citizens in the 21st century.

REFERENCES

de Rijcke, F. (2004, March). *Assessing ICT and learning.* Paper presented at the 2004 CoSN K-12 School Networking Conference, Arlington, VA.

Feicheng, M., and Cuihua, H. (2002, July). *Information literacy, education reform and the economy: China as a case study.* White Paper prepared for UNESCO, the U.S. National Commission on Libraries and Information Science, and the National Forum on Information Literacy, for use at the Information Literacy Meeting of Experts, Prague, Czech Republic. Available: http://www.nclis.gov/libinter/infolitconf&meet/papers/ma-fullpaper.pdf [accessed February 1, 2006].

Herz, J.C. (2002). The bandwidth capital of the world. *Wired Magazine, 10*(08), 1-4 .

Korea Institute of Curriculum and Evaluation. (2005). *National curriculum. II. Educational goals by school level. 3. The goals of high school education.* Available: http://www.kice.re.kr/kice/eng/info/info_2.jsp [accessed June 2006].

Korean Ministry of Education and Human Resources Development. (2003). *Adapting education to the information age.* Seoul, Korea: Korean Ministry of Education and Human Resources Development.

Kozma, R.B. (2005). National policies that connect ICT-based education reform to economic and social development. *Human Technology, 1,* 117–156.

National Commission on Excellence in Education. (1983). *A nation at risk.* Available: http://www.ed.gov/pubs/NatAtRisk/risk.html [accessed February 1, 2006].

National Research Council. (1999). *Being fluent with information technology.* Computer Science and Telecommunications Board, Washington, DC: National Academy Press.

National Research Council. (2006). *Rising above the gathering storm: Energizing and employing America for a brighter economic future.* Committee on Science, Engineering, and Public Policy, Washington, DC: The National Academies Press.

Partnership for 21st Century Skills. (2005). *The assessment of 21st century skills: The current landscape.* Available: http://www.21stcenturyskills.org/index.php?option=com_content&task=view&id=131&Itemid=103 [accessed February 1, 2006].

Snyder, L. (2006). *Fluency with information technology: Skills, concepts and capabilities.* 2nd ed. Boston, MA: Pearson Education.

Walton, S. (2005, January). *Key stage 3 onscreen test pilot.* London, England: Qualifications and Curriculum Authority.

Woods, H. (2004). *MCEETYA ICT in schools initiatives.* Presented to the Consortium for School Networking (CoSN) VIP delegation to Australia, 2004: Information Communications Technologies in Education Meeting, ICT in Schools Taskforce Secretariat. Australia: Ministerial Council on Education, Employment, Training and Youth Affairs.

2

Introduction

Information and communications technology (ICT) pervades virtually all domains of modern life—educational, professional, social, and personal. Yet although there have been numerous calls for linkages that enable ICT competencies acquired in one domain to benefit another, this goal has largely remained unrealized. In particular, while technology skills and applications at work could be greatly enhanced by earlier complementary learning at school—particularly in K–12 education, a formative and influential stage in a person's life—little progress has been made on such linkages.

At present, the curricula of most U.S. high schools focus on skills in the use of tools such as specific word-processing software or contemporary Internet search engines. Although these kinds of skills are certainly valuable—at least for a while—they comprise just one component, and the most rudimentary component, of ICT competencies. The high school years put little emphasis on underlying concepts of ICT, which will serve students far longer than familiarity with current but soon-obsolescent products and services. Nor do most high school curricula seriously address intellectual capabilities, which transcend ICT's current manifestations, for dealing with complexity.

Being Fluent with Information Technology[1] notes that a major constraint

---

[1]National Research Council. (1999). Washington, DC: National Academy Press.

in the teaching of ICT-related subjects is the factor of change. For example, when that report was published less than a decade ago, the World Wide Web had only recently become a public resource, and any discussion of ICT fluency just a few years earlier would not have included, or perhaps even envisioned, the browsing skills and other capabilities currently regarded as essential. Similarly, to shape curricula today that might be valid, say, 20 years hence would be mostly an exercise in futility.

Being Fluent thus emphasized life-long learning, which led to the report's well-received tripartite framework of ICT skills, ICT concepts, and intellectual capabilities. The skills enable the use of current technology. The concepts are essentially the foundation that allows students—and adults—to keep learning. And the capabilities effectively allow the wise use both of skills and concepts in the right way at the right time.

Under each of these three major components, moreover, *Being Fluent* identified 10 specific competencies (see Box 2-1). The committee members who developed the report intentionally limited themselves to this number because it forced them to choose the competencies they considered most important rather than generate an extensive list.

The report also stressed that "fluency" is not a synonym for "literacy." It is in fact much broader. Literacy is effectively embodied by the skills component, while the concepts and capabilities components take learners much further and deeper. As a result, the acquisition of literacy is a relatively straightforward process, whether in schools or elsewhere, but the teaching of fluency—imparting not only ICT skills but also concepts and capabilities—requires curricular change in which ICT is seen as more than a particular skill set, especially in the high schools.

Being Fluent advanced principles, centered on those sketched above, that apply to all of education, but it focused on the college (undergraduate) level. To address the specifics of ICT learning during the high school years would require an explicit effort to build on that report, which was the focus of the workshop that is the subject of this present report.

The workshop had three primary objectives: (1) to examine the need for updates to the ICT-fluency framework presented in the 1999 study; (2) to identify and analyze the most promising current efforts to provide in high schools many of the ICT competencies required not only in the workplace but also in people's day-to-day functioning as citizens; and (3) to consider what information or research is needed to inform efforts to help high school students develop ICT fluency.

To help ensure that the workshop would meet these objectives, the

---

BOX 2-1
Components of Fluency with Information Technology

Intellectual Capabilities
1. Engage in sustained reasoning.
2. Manage complexity.
3. Test a solution.
4. Manage problems in faulty solutions.
5. Organize and navigate information structures and evaluate information.
6. Collaborate.
7. Communicate to other audiences.
8. Expect the unexpected.
9. Anticipate changing technologies.
10. Think about information technology abstractly.

Information Technology Concepts
1. Computers.
2. Information systems.
3. Networks.
4. Digital representation of information.
5. Information organization.
6. Modeling and abstraction.
7. Algorithmic thinking and programming.
8. Universality.
9. Limitations of information technology.
10. Societal impact of information and information technology.

Information Technology Skills
1. Setting up a personal computer.
2. Using basic operating system features.
3. Using a word processor to create a text document.
4. Using a graphics and/or artwork package to create illustrations, slides, or other image-based expressions of ideas.
5. Connecting a computer to a network.
6. Using the Internet to find information and resources.
7. Using a computer to communicate with others.
8. Using a spreadsheet to model simple processes or financial tables.
9. Using a database system to set up and access useful information.
10. Using instructional materials to learn how to use new applications or features.

SOURCE: National Research Council (1999).

---

organizing committee invited four distinguished educators to prepare short papers for the workshop, and it developed a set of questions to guide its planning.

Karen Pittman of the Forum for Youth Investment, Paul Horwitz of the Concord Consortium, and Philip Bell of the University of Washington concentrated on learning. Specifically, they were asked to

- Discuss whether developments in ICT, the workplace, education, and society suggest that revisions—with a focus on expectations for high school students—to the initial framework of *Being Fluent* are needed.
- Reconsider the current curricular framework, both in terms of how it can be made appropriate for outlining high school graduation outcomes and how advances in ICT since 1999 can be taken into account.
- Emphasize research-based understanding of learning and effective learning environments, as well as how that knowledge might guide the revision of the *Being Fluent* framework.

Paul Resta of the University of Texas Learning and Technology Center concentrated on the workplace. He was asked to

- Reconsider the *Being Fluent* framework, both in terms of how it can be made appropriate for outlining high school graduation outcomes and how advances in ICT since 1999 can be taken into account.
- Focus particularly on changes in the workplace and their consequences for the level of ICT fluency needed in the current and future workforce.

Following the original "ground rules" of the study committee that developed the *Being Fluent* framework, all four authors were told that if they wanted to add a capability, concept, or skill to the framework, they could do so only if they eliminated an existing one. And if they did suggest the addition or removal of an item, they were asked to articulate the rationale for doing so. Lastly, the planning committee encouraged the authors to be forward-thinking, provocative, and yet realistic in the spirit of developing a framework suitable for high school outcomes in ICT. Their four papers appear as Appendixes A–D to this report.

The committee specified four critical questions for all participants in the workshop to consider in their presentations and interactions:

1. Do developments in ICT, the workplace, education, and society suggest that revisions to the initial framework of ICT fluency proposed by the *Being Fluent* are needed?
2. What do all high school students need to know and be able to do in ICT in order to be functional in society now and in the future?
3. What is the state of evidence about the effectiveness of current practices and courses aimed at enhancing ICT knowledge among high school students, with particular attention to the whole range of high school learners? What evaluations or other studies are available to assess the extent to which students participating in such programs become fluent with ICT (as defined in *Being Fluent* and in papers commissioned for the workshop)?
4. What further information or research is needed to reform efforts to help high school students develop competencies associated with all three capabilities of the ICT fluency framework, in the context of existing high school curricula?

These questions were intended to stimulate workshop discussion on what students should know when they leave high school and to challenge participants to look deeper into the problem—to suggest how students should gain these skills, concepts, and capabilities and through what learning mechanisms.

For example, does ICT need to be taught in special classes? Or can it be taught in the discipline-related classes? Because a good deal of the learning about it is presently occurring out of schools, another issue is whether ICT skills, concepts, and capabilities should be learned in school at all, or only partly in school. That is, what should be the tradeoff between formal and informal learning of ICT? Moreover, how will teachers become competent to teach ICT, especially when some of their students may be more knowledgeable than they are? Similarly, how will educators deal with the networked, nonlinear nature of ICT, especially as schools have traditionally been organized around a linear development of knowledge in specific subjects?

To elicit answers to these and related questions in as constructive a manner as possible, the workshop was organized into five sessions keyed respectively to the following five questions:

1. What makes ICT a critical topic in today's climate, and why is fluency in it essential?
2. What outcomes are needed? That is, how can ICT fluency be defined in practice?
3. What is currently being taught or learned?
4. How are the outcomes being measured?
5. What changes may be needed in the original ICT fluency framework of *Being Fluent*?

The next five chapters of this report summarize those five sessions. The questions that begin each chapter capture the major themes that were discussed during the session

Significant work on ICT education remains to be done, especially in high schools. By identifying what is known and unknown about the acquisition of ICT fluency during the high school years, the workshop was designed to move this work forward. The hope of its organizers and participants is that the workshop and this report will inform the National Science Foundation and other federal agencies, as well as policy makers, administrators, and faculty in high schools, community colleges, and undergraduate settings, as they consider ways of enhancing the ICT fluency of high school graduates.

3

ICT Fluency in the 21st Century

- *What do students need to know about information and communications technology (ICT) and how should that affect what happens in high schools?*
- *How can technology best be used as a multipurpose tool for learning and applying knowledge when its speed of development outpaces any given set of skills?*

The workshop's first session addressed the influence of ICT on the world today—and especially on the future—and why it is essential for students to leave high school well on the way toward acquiring ICT fluency. Speakers at this initial session therefore discussed the big picture: what the teaching of ICT fluency must take into account in order to be realistic, motivating, and effective.

They addressed the fast-changing nature of ICT and the consequent need not just to teach skills for using currently available technology but also to give students foundational understanding—both of the underlying information science and of associated problem-solving techniques. They addressed ICT's alteration of the world's socioeconomic landscape; incentives for acquiring ICT fluency, not only for abetting good citizenship and personal pleasure, but also for acquiring and keeping jobs; and broad metaphorical constructs by which teachers may tap into this potent phenomenon to inspire and enlighten students. And they suggested some means by which the teaching of ICT fluency may be integrated into high school curricula.

Presenters were William Wulf, president of the National Academy of Engineering and Christopher Dede, Timothy E. Wirth Professor of Learning Technologies at Harvard University. Respondents were Michael Eisenberg, dean of the Information School at the University of Washington and Bob Tinker, president of the Concord Consortium.

INEVITABLE CHANGE

William Wulf stated that he did not need to convince the audience of the importance of ICT—the workshop's purpose, after all, was to address *how* to teach it, not whether to teach it —but that he did want to emphasize a point in the welcoming statement of Lawrence Snyder, professor of computer science and engineering at the University of Washington and chair of the committee that produced *Being Fluent with Information Technology* (National Research Council, 1999). That point pertained to the inevitability of change in ICT, and thus the virtual impossibility of making accurate predictions about its manifestations beyond the near future. This reality has great implications for the *Being Fluent* framework, particularly regarding its list of contemporary skills, which by definition will change.

Having written his first computer program in 1959 and sent his first e-mail around 1970, Wulf said, "I feel like I've sat for 46 years on the 50-yard line, watching this technology change and watching its impact on society. And it has been absolutely fascinating"—especially to see how even the cognoscenti are often clueless about ICT's future course.

High on his list of wildly erroneous predictions are those of three of the field's most distinguished pioneers. Thomas Watson, as leader of IBM during the early 1950s, foresaw that the worldwide market for computers would be limited to merely six machines. "I observe," said Wulf in retrospect, "that my present car alone has more than six computers." Kenneth Olsen, founder of Digital Equipment Corporation, said in 1978—two years before the introduction of the IBM PC—that no one would ever want a computer in his or her home. And Bill Gates, the celebrated and highly successful head of Microsoft, predicted in the mid-1980s that no one would ever need more than 640 kilobytes of memory.

"Why were these people, each in a privileged position and thoroughly acquainted with the facts of the technology, so incredibly wrong?" asked

Wulf. "I have pondered this question for years and years, and the only explanation I can come up with is that in every case the person was assuming that the future was going to be like the present." The state-of-the-art computer available to Watson when he made his comment was the ponderous ENIAC (weighing 30 tons and occupying a space the size of a squash court), designed to calculate the ballistics of weaponry. Thus it was hardly a mass-market item. Olsen's model, though smaller, was still refrigerator-sized and in need of special conditions and constant maintenance—not a likely product for the home. And Gates's prediction was made at a time of no color, no graphics, or the various bells and whistles that computer users today take for granted and that require orders of magnitude more memory.

By basing their predictions so heavily on the present, these would-be prognosticators were led very much astray. "Don't make that same mistake," Wulf cautioned his audience. "The future is not going to be just a better version of today. It is, in some profoundly transformative way, going to be different from today."

Technological change has long been measured by Moore's Law, which states that a computer chip's number of transistors per unit area—and therefore its processing power—doubles about every 18 months. Although some people question whether this rapid rate of change can continue indefinitely—or at least, into their own future—they do so at their peril, said Wulf. It's best to assume that Moore's Law will continue to apply, which means no one should get too attached to the present ways of doing things.

If the law does hold for the next dozen years, Wulf said, we'll wind up with a microprocessor the size of the cross-section of a pin. While he couldn't predict the uses to which such a device would be put, he did argue that the profoundly larger keyboards and screens of today would be rendered obsolete. And the general-purpose personal computer—on which you run spreadsheets, do word-processing as we now know it, and browse the Internet—may be gone as well. "I don't know what will replace it," he said, "but if you stop and ask yourself how you would use such a tiny computer processing chip, it wouldn't be that way."

"It's not just that the underlying hardware changes fast," explained Wulf, "but as it does so, it enables more and more other things to change. And it's not just *how* we do things that will change, it's *what* we do that will change." This implies, he continued, that of the three competencies identified in *Being Fluent*, skill level is the most volatile and the most likely not to endure. "Skills will change. They will change rapidly, and they will change in discontinuous ways."

Thus, he concluded, his greatest priority for educators is that they teach the fundamentals of technology, which remain relevant with change and even help to affect it, and that they not limit themselves to teaching how to use particular technologies.

FACETS OF ICT FLUENCY

Chris Dede noted that Tom Friedman, in his 2005 book *The World Is Flat: A Brief History of the Twenty-First Century*,[1] recalls how when he was a boy his mother told him to eat his food because people all over the world wanted it. Now he tells his daughters to work hard—people all over the world want their jobs!

That situation results in large part from advances in ICT, Dede said. "We live in a very interesting time right now, because emerging technologies are doing three things at once, worldwide. They are shifting the kinds of knowledge and skills that society values in education. They are letting us use new and powerful methods of teaching and learning. And they are changing the characteristics of learners at every age." Dede lamented the disconnect between formal (academic) and informal learning, particularly for ICT. He indicated that what kids are doing outside of school—using sophisticated technologies and learning how to access information—is much more closely aligned to what knowledge workers do in industry than to what those kids are doing in school.

He agreed with Wulf that the technology is changing so fast that no one fully understands where it is going. "Whether you look at the device level, the application level, the level of media, or the level of infrastructures," Dede said, "on any given day somewhere in the news there is a significant advance that is reported." Yet he pointed out that this rapidity of change has not stopped many countries (other than our own) from making ICT—and ICT education—central elements of their planning. Though dealing with ICT is essentially to "have a tiger by the tail," he said, policy makers are still obligated to deal with it as best they can, which means taking the inevitability of change fully and realistically into account and, while taking note of potential problems, looking at the upside.

Dede cited *The New Division of Labor: How Computers Are Creating the Next Job Market*, a 2004 book by economists Frank Levy and Richard

---

[1]New York: Farrar, Straus, and Giroux.

Murnane,[2] as noting that while some jobs have disappeared because of ICT, others have flourished. Often, these latter jobs stress the skills that people can acquire but computers cannot. "When I think of myself in partnership with information communication technology," Dede said, "I often feel like the sorcerer who has a very fast but very dumb apprentice." It is through ICT fluency—and the productive, mutually reinforcing human/machine interactions it enables—that such partnerships may prosper, he maintained.

Dede offered three metaphors to illustrate his conceptions of ICT fluency. "Sometimes I feel like an artist who has a multidimensional palette," he said. For example, "in a course I teach every fall at Harvard we have eight different ways of interacting face to face and seven different ways of interacting across systems. When I come to a particular topic in the course, I typically think: Do I want to use groupware? Do I want to use a videoconference? Is this an asynchronous discussion? Is this something that best takes place in an immersive virtual environment? Or can it only be done face to face? "I know that each of those options shape their messages differently, and they shape how my students feel and how they interact with others. So as an 'instructional artist' I have to think about how to paint with that palette of media. That's a kind of ICT fluency."

Turning to his second metaphor, Dede said he sometimes feels as if he has an external virtual memory, made possible through technology, as a complement to his own internal memory—both of which operate in non-linear ways to represent knowledge and help him gain access to information. "How I take advantage, without literally losing my mind, of an external memory that complements my internal memory is also a kind of ICT fluency."

For his final metaphor, Dede referred to the multiuser virtual environments that he and his colleagues study. Many students regard these systems not just as learning environments but also as a theatre for the exploration of identity—especially among those who have come to think of themselves as academic losers. In a multiuser virtual environment, they can cast off that identity and express a different one.

"One of the most exciting things about ICT work," said Dede, "is how students who are underperforming in school often do as well as students who have much better academic records, have much better classroom be-

---

[2]Princeton, NJ: Princeton University Press.

haviors during conventional instruction, and much better class attendance. For the first time they are being taught in a way that not only reflects their learning style but also gives them the opportunity to let out an identity in a safe manner that has been repressed for them." This too, Dede maintained, is a kind of ICT fluency.

But he stressed that these three metaphors, and others, are just his own way of dealing with the complex construct called ICT. Other people may develop their own to suit their individual circumstances and styles. "As each of us thinks about the metaphors that reflect our own experience, or our children's experience, it is going to help us understand how to get all the parts of ICT fluency together."

As a parting thought, Dede said that while he is interested in ICT in its own right, he also sees wrestling with its uses and implications as "a prelude to the Faustian dilemma" that is coming with biotechnology. "Right now we are exploring the kinds of complementary relationships we can have with devices, tools, media, applications, and infrastructures as we 'cybernate' our lives. We try to understand what that means for us and for society— where it's a step forward, and where at times it's a step back. Thus, ICT fluency may sometimes mean: *Don't* do this with ICT. So my hope is that when we gain the power, through biotechnology, not just to manipulate an external memory but also our own memory and not just a virtual identity but our own bodies, we will by then have learned enough lessons from our ICT fluency experiences to know what to do and what not to do."

IT'S NOT JUST THE TECHNOLOGY

Michael Eisenberg agreed with both of the presenters on the rapidity and impact of technological change that now characterize society. Consider, he said, how the World Wide Web, in just a decade, has so broadly affected our lives. "The next generation, or generations, of technology will likely be about something just as profound, if not more profound," said Eisenberg. Like the two earlier presenters, he confessed to not having a crystal ball for seeing what that will be, but he suggested that "it might very well be a combination of the digital and the biological." In any case, he said, "I have a strong suspicion that we are going to see wave after wave of this, so I don't think we should get too comfortable."

Yet it would be a serious mistake, Eisenberg insisted, for educators to deal with the undeniable effects of technological change by focusing just on technology. "It's not about the technology," he said. "It's about people. It's about people's needs. It's about productivity. It's about money: we are a capitalist society, and a lot of what is driving technology is our businesses and individuals trying to make money."

"It's also about fun", Eisenberg said. "Technology today is about fun. People search the Web for fun."

Fun applies not only to recreation but also to just about any pursuit that gratifyingly engages the human mind. That's why, Eisenberg predicted, the *Being Fluent* framework will change least in terms of intellectual capabilities. The contemporary skills will change the most, as obsolescent tools are succeeded by better ones. And the foundational concepts will change as ICT itself changes. But the basic attributes that enable people to apply ICT in complex and sustained situations, and to practice higher-level thinking in the context of ICT, will stay pretty much the same as the technology undergoes evolution or even revolution.

Nevertheless, people need to stay up-to-date in order to orchestrate the laundry lists of skills, concepts, and capabilities for students' benefit. In that spirit, he noted, "I love Chris Dede's metaphor of the teacher as instructional artist."

Eisenberg expressed confidence in students and issued a challenge to their teachers. "There is something special about growing up in this country—a free and open environment where we can imagine and do just about anything. So I'm not worried about America's youth. As an educator, I just want to put them in a position to succeed."

DEEPENING THE ICT EXPERIENCE

Bob Tinker offered his own challenge to educators, prompted by what he sees as the "over-romanticizing" of kids' use of technology. "They are not a species separate from us, and they are just learning, too," Tinker said. "In many cases, I have observed that students' use of technology, which may be very broad, can be very shallow."

For example, having long watched kids playing with Sims software, he concluded that they tend to focus on the 3-D construction aspects of the situation rather than on the underlying mathematical model that is the basis of much more profound learning. Similarly, while some people use spreadsheet software to build their own models, a great many others simply put numbers into the existing cells. Thus, Tinker observed, ICT skills don't necessarily get to higher-level skills without explicit teacher intervention. "It's important," he said, "to think about what it is we want to teach."

Tinker suggested that one useful path to more in-depth ICT learning would be its acquisition as part of science, technology, engineering, and mathematics (STEM) learning. Devising applications of ICT for that purpose would improve the quality of these tools, and they in turn would improve STEM education. He cited as example his own work with the Kids' Network, in which e-mail was the basis not only for the sharing of data but also for students' active collaboration and intellectual development. More generally, ICT can also make possible "modification, customization, construction, and adaptation, which can really enrich STEM education overall," he said.

At the moment, however, while the sophistication of technology is growing rapidly, "the educational use of technology is certainly not," said Tinker. "Too often, when computers are used in education the kids are passive; they are not taking advantage of the power that is sitting right in front of them." More fundamentally, he added, is that the teachers themselves are not making good use of these technologies, and consequently "are throwing away a tremendous resource."

One of the reasons for this, Tinker suggested, "is that our dissemination model for ICT is wrong. There simply isn't enough money in the system to lubricate the corporation—the private business models that are necessary for really sophisticated use of ICT. We just get the simplest things. And I think the model has to go over to open-source applications as well as open-source operating systems."

Another big problem, he said, is teachers' professional development. "We have to devote significant resources to it, and significant resources to doing it well"—especially if we decide to put ICT skills into the high school curriculum by building it into STEM education."

THINK GLOBALLY, ACT LOCALLY

Some of the speakers referred to this kick-off session of the workshop as "the view from 50,000 feet." Audience members, many of them educators with extensive high school teaching experience, responded in kind—and with passion. Some of these commentaries related directly to the goal of ICT fluency, but most put ICT fluency into a larger educational context or addressed even bigger big-picture issues that underlie not just ICT but virtually all of K–12 education.

Eric Klopfer, director of the MIT Teacher Education Program, agreed with Bob Tinker that people sometimes over-romanticize the vision of what kids do with technology and that in fact their uses are often super-ficial. "Still, in many cases this is more than we are asking them to do in schools," he said, "and it's something we should try to build on." At the same time, Klopfer added, we need to help change "kid culture," at least in the United States, to render it more amenable to learning in general and to gaining ICT fluency in particular—in contrast to the literacy that so many kids already have. "Students should *want* to learn those skills," he said. But the challenge is considerable. He quoted Tom Friedman: "In Japan, Bill Gates is their Britney Spears. In this country, Britney Spears is our Britney Spears."[3]

Deborah Boisvert, director of the National Science Foundation IT Center at the University of Massachusetts, Boston, similarly stressed the need "to really challenge education to create an environment for learning." She specifically contrasted the traditionally solitary type of educational en-vironment in the United States, one that is much less social than in many other countries. "I remember a demonstration that we had done with a very exciting collaborative network environment," she said, "and the [U.S.] teachers came back and said, 'Omigosh, we can't deal with this, because all the kids are cheating!' "

Ralph Coppola, director of worldwide education at the Parametric Technology Corporation, reminded the audience that "technology and soft-ware tools are a means to an end, not an end in themselves." Moreover, some of those ends can be ambitious indeed. In the Chicago public schools, he reported, some 90–95 percent of the students who graduate are not ready for college. "In dealing with this issue of a large fraction of our public school population who are not succeeding with the traditional methodol-ogy being employed," he said, "perhaps we can use an alternative portal to the academic enterprise—and perhaps that portal can be ICT."

Steve Robinson, a high school teacher from Eugene, Oregon, currently on a one-year leave as an Albert Einstein Fellow to work for Senator Barack Obama, pointed out that the diversity of students can confound the teach-ing of ICT. "I have students who need to power down to come to school, and I have students who have never seen a computer before." Another critical challenge, he said, is teacher competency in ICT. Few educators are qualified, "not because they are bad teachers but because they just haven't

---

[3] *The World Is Flat: A Brief History of the Twenty-First Century.* (2005). New York: Farrar, Straus, and Giroux.

been trained in this area." The task often goes to biology or math teachers simply by default, whether they are "ICT gurus" or not. Robinson thus asked whether any state teachers' colleges have made teaching about ICT an integral part of their curriculum.

Bette Manchester, director of special projects at the Maine Department of Education, made a similar point while raising the stakes. "Sorting out the needed skills and competencies, whether they be of the children or of the adults," will be moot, she said, "if you have leaders and principals and superintendents who are unable, or don't have any idea how, to create a learning organization inside a school. Leadership is something that needs to be attended to."

Isa Zimmerman, a professor at Lesley University in Cambridge, Massachusetts, and a former high school principal and superintendent of schools, cited a problem that she said can tie the hands of even the most competent of educational leaders—community resistance to change. "So although I am one of those people who resents being told what to do, I have on many occasions appreciated a piece of legislation that enabled me to say: 'You have to do it, because that is what the law says.' " In the absence of such forcings, she said, a community often lacks the political will, which means that resources to effect change will be scarce. "Things won't change," she said, "unless we change the political climate."

Jim Stanton described his work at the Southwest Regional Employment Board in Boston, Massachusetts, as "developing partnerships between some of the state's larger corporations and an array of public schools specifically around STEM programs." And in his comments he raised the issue of political will to the national level. "One of my very great concerns here is the fundamental disconnect," he said, "between what is happening in public education and what is happening in our economy, and there is an order-of-magnitude difference." Unless we redouble our efforts in the United States around STEM-career education in general and the teaching of ICT fluency in particular, said Stanton, businesses will have to look elsewhere for their workers.

Margaret Honey, vice president of the Educational Development Center and chair of the workshop, summarized the audience's comments. Many of those who spoke, she said, suggested that education simply has not changed in response to the realities of technology and that we are stuck in 20th-century education practices. "What some of you are asking us to do is to come up with different strategies for acknowledging, recognizing, and encouraging the development of people's competencies." Alongside these challenges, Dr. Honey suggested, are the issues of equity and access, which need to be acknowledged in any discussion of ICT and education. She reminded the audience that Karen's Pittman's paper (see Appendix A) for the meeting noted that roughly one-third of all teenagers in the United States do not graduate from high school (50 percent of all teens of color do not graduate).

Honey pointed out that while there are some very real disconnects in all of our professional contexts, at this workshop we want to keep our focus on the appropriateness of the ICT fluency framework as a template to guide how ICT is operationalized in the high schools. "This meeting is really about creating a blueprint to help people move forward," she concluded.

4

Perspectives on High Schools

- *What information and communications technology (ICT)-related outcomes are needed from K–12 education?*
- *Why is it important to distinguish between literacy and fluency?*
- *What is the relationship between ICT fluency and today's most valued job skills?*

This session's speakers agreed that while learning particular technical skills associated with contemporary technology is essential at any time, much more important over the long run is learning how to learn. Given that technologies and their applications change rapidly, and sometimes radically, students need to be prepared for lifelong learning. Teachers must encourage and guide them so that they acquire the foundations of such competencies by the time they leave high school.

Similarly, participants in the session emphasized the need to acquire broad skills that not only are obsolescence-proof but also happen to be perennially desired by employers. The ability to communicate, collaborate, think critically, deal with ambiguity, and solve problems—to possess, that is, the elements of fluency—were repeatedly cited as essentials for the workplace. Nuts-and-bolts technical skills are never unimportant, of course, but given possession of the broader capacities, they are relatively easy to acquire—and to relearn as situations inevitably change.

Presenters were Wendy Hawkins, executive director of the Intel Foundation; Thomas N. Applegate, executive dean of Austin Community College, Texas; and Karen Bruett, director of education and community initiatives at Dell, Inc. Respondents were Daniel Gohl, principal of McKinley Technical High School, Washington, DC, and Julia Fallon, program developer for technical education, Office of the Superintendent of Public Instruction, Washington State.

ALL THAT THEY CAN BE

High school students often have more familiarity with current computer and information technology—a greater literacy—than do their teachers, Wendy Hawkins noted. Thus, if they are to help young people acquire ICT *fluency*, teachers and those in the business of educating teachers must adjust their attitudes and approaches.

As an analogy, Hawkins described her recent quest to correct an omission from childhood—to learn to play the piano. She took piano lessons and diligently applied herself, playing two hours a day for some five years. "But it became increasingly clear to me," she said, "that I was never going to be able to play the piano the way that eight-year-olds would. There are things that get into your 'muscle memory'—that are programmed into your brain in those early years—that an adult will never be able to catch up with."

Similarly, she suggested, "the notion that we are going to retrain our teaching workforce to be able to keep up with kids who were born to this technology, who were immersed in it practically from day one, is nonsense." We've got to make our teachers feel comfortable with that "fact of life," she said, and direct them instead to motivate and guide students to build on their ICT foundations so that they may become as effective they can be.

An effort in that pedagogical direction, according to Hawkins, is Intel's Teach to the Future Program for providing teacher professional development. This hands-on, face-to-face, 40-hour course, she said, trains teachers to apply the tools of technology in classrooms in meaningful ways and to transform their teaching roles from central source of knowledge to enabler of students in their own individualized quests for knowledge. The idea is to place students at the center and encourage them to become lifelong learners, not only for keeping up with technology but also for using it as creatively and effectively as possible. This "quite transformative" training program, she said, has now been offered in 47 countries, and 3 million teachers have completed it.

Another fact of life, said Hawkins, is that schools in the United States will never have the money to keep up with the business world, technologically speaking. Schools will not, at any time, boast state-of-the-art, cutting-edge systems in its classrooms. But "that does not excuse us," she said, "from requiring that kids understand how to use the technology or from requiring of ourselves that we give them as much opportunity as we can."

A third fact of life, she said, is that the education community must not aim too low—say, by gearing its ICT programs to kids who can't afford computers in their homes. Higher standards will raise expectations and inspire better performance by schools and students alike. "We who are in this room today," said Hawkins, "are obligated to set the bar so that it makes them successful, not at a place where it's easy for them to step over it. This isn't a limbo game. It's the high hurdles."

She cited another Intel program called Computer Clubhouse that aims to help students respond to higher ICT standards. These computer labs, designed in collaboration with Boston's Museum of Science and the Massachusetts Institute of Technology, typically offer underserved inner-city youth "the opportunity to put their hands on the best technology around," said Hawkins. "It turns them loose to dive in, become immersed in the technology, and do in-depth work in the kinds of things that really grab kids," such as the arts—making their own music and burning CDs— and graphic design and video.

A broader goal for the program, she added, is that this informal education route will help pull kids back into the formal education environment. And that goal, according to Hawkins, is being met: "It has been as successful in the slums of New Delhi as in inner-city Chicago as in the Soweto townships of South Africa."

Intel is investing some $100 million each year in programs of this sort, Hawkins said, because "we are really, really concerned about the state of education and whether our children and grandchildren are going to be prepared" for the demanding, productive, and high-paying jobs of the not-so-distant future. For example, she lamented that while engineers in the United States are being trained in fewer and fewer numbers, schools around the world—whether in China, Nigeria, or Brazil; whether in countries with fully mature economies, as in Western Europe; or whether in countries in the early stages of development, as in sub-Saharan Africa—are absorbing technology as fast as they can. "Technology is moving in, and their expectations for their kids are moving sky high," said Hawkins. "They are going to eat our lunch unless we keep ahead."

CONTINUALLY LEARNING AND ADAPTING

Thomas Applegate noted that in his field of career and technical education, formerly called "vocational education," programs are based on standards set by business and industry. In the licensed occupations, such as nursing, standards are straightforwardly prescribed by law or board policy. Outside the licensed occupations, however, answering the question of "What are the correct standards?" becomes more abstract and subject to shifting needs. Educating young people for business and industry thus obliges teachers to take a broad view by imparting to their students not only contemporary skills but also the ability to learn new ones later on.

The primacy of being skilled (as opposed to unskilled) may be seen by the changes, over the past 55 years, in the composition of the U.S. workforce, Applegate said. In 1950, the U.S. Department of Labor said that 20 percent of the country's jobs required a baccalaureate degree, 5 percent required technical training, and 75 percent were basically unskilled manual labor kinds of jobs. But in 2005, while the percentage of jobs requiring a baccalaureate degree remained at 20 percent, 70 percent of the jobs demanded technical preparation, and only 10 percent were unskilled.

And it's not only skills that are important, Applegate maintained, but their relevance. "In earlier times, students could take one of three courses of study: college prep, which prepared them for college; vocational education, which prepared them for a job; or general education, which essentially prepared them for nothing," he said. "But the thinking in career and technical education today is that it's all about job preparation *and* further education, not job preparation *or* further education." Given how quickly the world is changing, with the requisite skills changing along with it, "truly the 20 percent and the 70 percent of the jobs that require technical skills also require education beyond high school." For that reason, Applegate said, employers want people who not only have the technical skills needed for the job but also the foundational skills, which include ICT fluency, for continually learning and adapting.

As most teachers know, education systems are slow to respond to such realities, he observed. For example, biology, chemistry, and physics began being taught in that sequence, some 100 years ago, simply because it was alphabetic, and they are still taught that way. Nevertheless, he suggested, teachers do have options with respect to preparing students for careers and the ever-changing requirements they will face.

In current technical education, "when you teach a concept, you must teach it in context and with rigor. It's the combination of concept, context, and rigor that will move our students from the skills in use today to the skills they will need tomorrow, many of which are currently unknown."

DOING IT BETTER, CHEAPER, AND FASTER

Karen Bruett, a past chair and long-time member of the Partnership for 21st Century Skills (and of its predecessor organization, the CEO Forum on Education Technology), covered three basic topics in her talk: the staffing needs of corporations today, how companies tend to measure and evaluate their human resources, and the Partnership's view of how to prepare young people accordingly.

The contemporary workplace, said Bruett, is really different from what it was during most of the 20th century. For example, in the 1950s the organizational structure of the corporation, and of most other institutions, was very hierarchical. People at the top would not just give direction but tell employees what to do, virtually to the level of daily individual tasks.

"That world doesn't exist anymore," said Bruett. "Direction at a corporation today is no longer task-specific but instead is very broad. So you need employees who can understand how to take an end-game objective and figure out for themselves the best way and the best tasks for achieving that objective. Companies are not counting on managers to figure this out. This is a world where the front-line employee more and more is empowered—and expected—to make those decisions."

Thus, Dell recently opened a new manufacturing facility—its largest worldwide—in North Carolina, she said, mainly because of the sophistication and versatility of local workers. The state has an outstanding K–12 education system, numerous universities that the company can draw on, and a population that understands manufacturing from its experience with the textile industry. "The ability to attract a skilled workforce was very important to us," she said. "We need people who are flexible, adaptable, know how to adjust to change, find their own work, and do process improvement. Employees on our manufacturing floor not only have to be able to build anywhere from 15 to 20 different products but, because they are closest to where the job is being done, help us figure out how to do it better, cheaper, and faster."

In evaluating people for hiring or promotion, Bruett said, companies essentially ask three main questions: Are you able to set directions? Are you able to align and motivate others? And are you able to deliver results? If so, the person is likely to have "strategic agility"—the capacity to build effective teams and especially to deal with ambiguity. The latter, she said, is "our number-one core competency at Dell, and probably in any technology organization, because what you learned yesterday is likely to be obsolete three months from now."

In terms of educating people to enter such a working world, the priorities of even just a few years ago are way off, Bruett noted. In the past it was all about the computer-to-student ratio—the purported need for x computers in every classroom. "But after the schools got connected accordingly, we realized that we were missing the boat—even though some of the kids were learning how to use the computers, we hadn't even begun to tap the potential of what technology can do. And that is its ability to improve collaboration, cooperation, and teamwork and help develop people who are analytical thinkers and problem solvers."

Bruett indicated that the kind of abilities that Dell as a corporation values do not automatically happen by having every student learn how to use Excel and PowerPoint. While it is important to understand how to use technology, its real power is in helping students become more collaborative, better critical thinkers, and more global in their perspective. Thus, in promoting the use of ICT in the classroom, Bruett said, "you never hear the Partnership for 21st Century Skills talk about technology in general or computers in particular. What you do hear us talk about are things like ICT literacy, thinking and problem-solving, interpersonal and self-direction skills, and the ability to be a lifelong learner. And we believe technology is a wonderful tool to promote those characteristics."

In a related point, the Concord Consortium's Paul Horwitz identifies in his paper (see Appendix B) an element of communications literacy by contrasting the reading of a book, a scholarly article, or even a newspaper with reading text on a computer. He indicates that to "read" a computer, students need to learn how to follow hypertext links without getting lost or forgetting what their original intent was: they need to master a certain form of nonlinear thinking.

Horwitz also suggests that 21st-century students need to know something about computer-based modeling in applications ranging from global climate change to the behavior of airfoils. He believes that they do not need to know how to build such models or even how to employ them, but they should know that they exist, how they are used, and what their limitations are. Moreover, Horwitz makes the case that ICT fluency for students has to include developing their awareness of the potential misuse of databases involving personal information.

GETTING MORE POINTS OF VIEW

The acquisition of ICT fluency, as opposed to ICT literacy, is very much in the spirit of what employers are asking of employees, said respondent Daniel Gohl. "Literacy is functional," he said, while "fluency is expressive, adaptive, and can deal with ambiguity."

He cited two major points related to the goal of cultivating such fluency. One is that just as colleges and businesses have certain requirements or expectations for high school graduates, it is also important—especially regarding ICT, to which exposure often begins at a very young age—to articulate what students need to have when *entering* high school. This is actually the law, he said, as the No Child Left Behind Act requires local jurisdictions to make explicit what eighth-graders can do in technology.

Gohl's second point was that to help assure the relevance stressed by Applegate, teaching of ICT fluency must be embedded in the core curriculum. "It must be tied to the four years of English, the three years of math, the three years of social studies, the three units of science, and foreign languages." he said. "If we are expecting separate courses to do it, they will always be optional."

Transcending the issue of the context in which ICT is taught is the basic purpose of that learning, Gohl said. While schools are often criticized for changing from what they were in the past, for him they have not been changing enough. The important question today, said Gohl, is why schools do not more closely resemble workplaces. Moreover, he maintained, the traditional dichotomy between college preparation and work preparation no longer applies.

He also agreed with the panel's speakers that all who enter the workforce will have to know how to keep learning throughout their careers, given the idiosyncrasy of skills in any particular field, along with the inevitable need to soon acquire new ones. And learning how to learn must necessary be rigorous—that is, intense. Defining intensity as "repeated iterations at increasing complexity," Gohl said "we must state what it is students are expected to get, how teachers are to teach it, and then use assessments that are aligned with the fluency frameworks." He added that in recognition of the working world's dynamism, "we must also change what students do from year to year to train them to be used to change. It is not a static script."

Gohl concluded with a recommendation posed as a question, which he invited the panel and audience to answer, regarding assessment. "I've done calculations showing that some 1,500 forms of assessment are done during four years of high school, and almost every time they are submitted to one person for review. But we know that performance in the world of work, and academic success, are in fact collectively appraised. How can we use ICT to ensure multiple forms of assessment in high school so that feedback is more refined?"

He suggested such collective evaluation would increase the degree of relevance because feedback on students' work would no longer be determined by the response or lack of it, of a single teacher; and students would be less likely to conclude that they are engaged in meaningless tasks. Collective evaluation in high school would also be more akin to future assessments on the job. "When people enter the workforce," Gohl said, "they know that if they don't perform they will fail and lose their job. We need schools to have a similar kind of public performance. And technology allows us to communicate what is going on."

Applegate agreed, noting that "when one person is the sole evaluator or is the content expert, then everything in a classroom depends on how that person teaches." As an example, he cited his experience with the Pythagorean theorem (in a right triangle, the three sides a, b, and c have the relationship $a^2 + b^2 = c^2$). "I learned it in high school, I memorized it, I didn't know what the heck it was good for, and I never used it—until, years later, I was in a construction-trades class one day with a teacher who showed how it could determine whether a wall is square to the floor. That teacher was creative and taught in context," Applegate said. "But if only one teacher evaluates the work, how do we know that this teacher is being creative and teaching contextually?" With multiple people looking at a student's work, disseminated through technology, the probability is considerably higher that at least some of the evaluators will have that gift.

Bruett cited just such a technology-based process at Dell, called "360," that not only provides collective evaluation to employees from managers but is multidirectional—"well rounded"—as its name implies. It enables peers to evaluate employees and employees to evaluate managers. Such feedback is currently being done in some schools in the context of project-based learning, she added. "I also think it becomes especially interesting when the students provide evaluation feedback to the teachers, because too often the students are only on the receiving end. But this way they come to understand that they have a responsibility for helping the teacher improve and that they actually have something valuable to say about it. We need to get more points of view, and technology can make it possible in a low-risk, safe environment for all concerned."

Paul Horwitz pointed out that although collective assessments are desirable they are not necessarily practical. What with all the students in a class (or employees in a workplace) and all their evaluators, the evaluation process itself—especially when it involves numerous and often subtle traits such as those involved in collaboration and problem-solving—becomes complex and not usually based on direct observation. So his organization has been "experimenting over the last several years with automated analyses of these kinds of data," Horwitz said, "as an example of how technology can help solve the problems that it raises." Such evaluations, moreover, are available in real time as people are working.

Ralph Coppola of the Parametric Technology Corporation cited a similar, Web-based tool, called Precision Learning that his company uses in its training programs. "What happens," he said, "is that people get immediate feedback about their progress in the various aspects of a course. They learn which things they need to devote more attention to, and they can reallocate resources and time very rapidly, precisely, and effectively."

With regard to collective assessments, Diane Baxter of the San Diego Supercomputer Center noted that at the middle and elementary school levels, more and more teachers are asking kids to review each other's work, with the teachers often evaluating the comments to see how well the students are reviewing. This process is greatly facilitated by technology, she pointed out. For example, the "track changes" function avoids any confusion resulting from young people's sometimes hard-to-read handwriting.

Mary Downs of the Institute of Museum and Library Services (an independent federal agency) stressed "the continuum of development of technology skills" from K–12 to colleges to the workplace, which highlights the need for lifelong learning. She pointed out as well the important complementary role of "informal learning environments" such as libraries, museums, and community centers. "If corporations assume responsibility to assist" in developing ICT fluency, she said, "their collaboration with community centers will help assure that this sort of learning can take place."

J. Linda Williams, director of library media services for Anne Arundel County (Maryland) Public Schools, noted that assessments of students' work, especially with respect to problem solving and critical thinking, could derive as well from these informal learning environments—particularly libraries. In seeking collective evaluations, she said, "don't forget about your library media specialist, teacher-librarian, or whatever they are called in your area. They teach problem solving, both to students and teachers, and they are important collaborators in teaching students how to think and how to learn."

Philip Sumida of Maine Township (Illinois) High School West agreed with Downs on the importance of informal learning environments, and he referred participants to the paper by Karen Pittman (see Appendix A), which developed that idea. He also underscored Williams's advocacy of librarians as worthy collaborators. In that spirit, he quoted Michael Eisenberg's earlier remark, "We are all slowly becoming librarians."

TURNING TEACHERS ON

"You don't teach fluency; rather, students *become* fluent," said respondent Julia Fallon. She recounted how one professor in college "pulled me across the line" from mere literacy with spreadsheets, word processing, and the like into the beginnings of ICT fluency. The difference, she said, was in encouraging exploration and self-learning. "By being allowed to tinker, I was motivated to ask myself 'How do I make this work for me?'"

Similarly, she said, "kids don't go around saying 'technology, technology, technology' or tell themselves 'Omigosh, I'm doing math.' It's all together, and we need to show students how it works all together. We teach them foundational skills, and then they are able to tinker and use those tools. They may use them in ways we don't even envision, which is the idea. And they may ask for help from peers or collaborate on a school project. We want to give them enough of a skill set so that they can craft and innovate for themselves in the future."

But a confounding factor for teachers at present, she noted, is that they must grapple with a multiplicity of standards and requirements at the state and national levels. "It gets confusing," she said, "and I want to know if there will be a unifying framework so that we can see it and know where it all comes together, or if there will at least be a place for common definitions." Essentially, Fallon said, we need to be using the same language when we are talking about ICT, literacy, and fluency.

Bruett agreed on the desirability of "a common language and a framework broad enough to be an umbrella for many different initiatives," and she referred to past, but unsuccessful, efforts to do just that. There are just too many different organizations in the education community, she said, "to get words that would work for everybody."

But there is no reason why, in the interest of high school reform, we can't get all stakeholders together to agree on the "end product," said Bruett. "We are all interested, after all, in what this kid should look like when coming out of school and what he or she should be ready to do. This is perhaps the kind of universal framework on which we *can* all agree. On exactly how to get there, agreement is rarely possible. But by focusing on the end game we have a much better chance of commonality and driving toward the same thing."

With respect to "end game," Jean Moon, director of the National Academies' Board on Science Education, observed that although there are multiple standards in multiple subjects, Bruett's recommendations referred not to the discrete levels that standards usually address. She instead spoke in more holistic terms around competencies. Thus, Moon asked her to pick the top five or so competencies that seem to cut across the work environment and could bridge back to high schools and middle schools. "What might those competencies be?" Moon asked. "And how might you get us started down this path of looking at things more broadly?"

Bruett put communication at the top of her list. "That's the one thing that is always evaluated," she said. "In every interview and in every job, communication skills are critical, and that's never going to change." She also cited problem solving and critical thinking: "We are looking for people who can figure out the next big thing, the way to do what we do better, the way to do what we do less expensively". Next is the ability to deal with ambiguity: "When there is no one road to the answer, it is so important to focus on what you want to accomplish at the end and then pick your right path for getting there". Also on the list are global awareness and global literacy: "Many organizations today function in collaborative global networks of teams of people working across the world to solve problems."

Hawkins elaborated on qualities that comprise problem-solving. It is not just finding solutions per se, she said, but also a facility to address the right problem and to ask the right question in the first place. It is as important to look at data and understand them, she said, as well as evaluate them.

Diane Baxter of the San Diego Supercomputer Center and Jennifer Coughlin of the U.S. Department of Energy's Office of Science raised the issue of teacher education and teacher leadership for implementing such goals. Teachers are not much accustomed to change, she observed, even though restructuring is fast becoming endemic to so many organizations, and teachers are not necessarily comfortable with ICT to begin with.

Hawkins noted that Intel has provided teachers with training "that gives them confidence and gets them over the hurdle of being afraid to use technology for fear of looking dumb in front of their students." The idea, she said, is to motivate teachers not only to effect change in their own classrooms but also to become advocates for inspiring other teachers, as well as administrators, in their school.

Fallon said that she tries to do much the same thing in her own job, where she sometimes refers to herself as a "technology drug dealer" because she turns teachers on to some exhilarating revelations—that they can allow themselves to look human in front of their class and that they actually have a lot more facility with technology and comfort with change than they thought they had. "We try to demystify," she said. "'We are not asking you to do rocket science,' I tell teachers. 'We are asking you do to some very simple things with some tools that convey the content you are trying to get across.'" And more often than not, Fallon added, "all of a sudden you start to see this little light bulb in their head turn on, and it's very exciting for me."

Susan Yoon from the University of Pennsylvania cited the need to bridge the traditional separation between formal classroom-learning environments and informal learning places, where students grow increasingly proficient in their knowledge and use of technology. We should be taking a look at what students do outside of school, she said, and trying to apply those lessons to classrooms. Yoon's remarks were consistent with the observation by Philip Bell, in his paper for this meeting (see Appendix C), that ICT has become fully integrated into the texture of young people's routine daily activities.

But in his paper (see Appendix B), Horwitz maintained that while kids' learning of ICT competencies outside of school is inevitable and desirable, this important niche is unlikely to be duplicated in the more formal school environments. Learning the fundamentals of operating technology is not likely to ever be part of the core curriculum of school he suggested, nor should it be.

5

What Are High School
Students Learning?
Where and How Are They Learning It?

- *In what ways might information and communications technology (ICT) help to redefine the outcomes, structures, and environments of high schools?*
- *What factors influence how high school students come to know and use ICT?*
- *What might be the social dimensions of ICT fluency?*

This session explored specific strategies and programs for cultivating ICT fluency among high school students. Speakers detailed many of the essential elements of success for gaining access to ICT and using it creatively and effectively in learning. They suggested how to build schools of the future from scratch and how to transform today's schools into schools of the future. And they stressed that while none of this could be done without technology, more important was strong school leadership and teamwork, teacher and student participation in planning, teacher and student collaboration, and school environments that are supportive both of independent and interdependent learning.

Throughout the session, several issues were stressed: the need to embed ICT across the high school curriculum (rather than its being an isolated subject); why some schools make progress in adopting ICT and using it wisely while others do not; how teachers and administrators could learn from successful noneducational organizations; the value of informal and project-based learning; and dealing with external impediments while fostering approaches within the schools that are as productive as possible.

Presenters were Mary Cullinane, academic program manager at Microsoft's School of the Future Program; Betty Manchester, director of special projects at the Maine Department of Education; and Vera Michalchik, a research social scientist at SRI's Center for Technology Learning. Respondents were Joyce Malyn-Smith, director of strategic initiatives at the Education Development Center and Philip Sumida, a physics instructor at the Maine Township High School West (Des Plaines, Illinois) and a former member of the National Research Council's Teacher Advisory Council.

ANSWERING THE CRITICAL QUESTIONS

Mary Cullinane described a "school of the future" project in which Microsoft is a lead collaborator for the School District of Philadelphia. Scheduled to open in September 2006, this school will be a neighborhood high school for 750 local students. "It's not focused on math and science, and it's not focused on the arts," she said. "We are trying to demonstrate the norm in urban education, not the extraordinary."

Cullinane recounted the "critical questions" that she and her fellow team members asked themselves during their planning for the school, and she suggested that these questions are pertinent as well to cultivating ICT fluency among students at any high school.

- *What are we trying to create?* The high school of the future, Cullinane said, should have a learning environment that is *continuous* ("not dependent on time and place"); *relevant* ("in its materials, curriculum, and outputs"); and *adaptive* ("allowing us to address the individual student").
- *Who are we creating it for?* A school ultimately serves students' future workplaces. It should graduate young people well prepared for success, both in building their own careers and in advancing their organizations' values—and value to society. But for a school to realize such objectives, she said, it must first and foremost know its students.
- *How will you organize your work?* "Key areas of development that we are working on in the school of the future," said Cullinane, include "innovation in the areas of building design, IT (information tech-

nology) architecture, community engagement, and instruction." These areas will be directly linked to learning outcomes, articulated by the schools' educators that comprise the basic elements for cultivating student skills.

- *What is going to guide your journey?* Cullinane cited the need for a framework and a well-defined process for building a school, but she urged selectivity. "You need to balance," she said. "There is a lot of process out in the world, not a lot of doing. And we need to make sure we don't get too process heavy."

- *What will allow you to be successful?* Borrowing the term "critical success factor" from the working world, Cullinane asked: "Can you identify your critical success factors when you talk about the types of students you want to see graduated? What are the things that you absolutely have to have in order for you to yield the outcome you want?" Here, too, she urged selectivity: "In education, everything seems to be critical," she said. But given the limits on time and resources, "everything *can't* be critical."

- *What assets do you need to build in order to get where you want to go?* Those assets, Cullinane said, should align with your critical success factors. In that regard, educators might well borrow again from industry. She offered as example Microsoft's "competency wheel"—a Web-based tool, referencing the organization's approximately 30 core competencies, that is designed to assist employees' professional growth. "As soon as I saw that tool," she said. "I thought 'That's what we should have had in education.' So now I'm building a school-of-the-future competency wheel." Cullinane said that the project team is now working with educators from around the world to help them identify what those competencies should be for high school students and the resources and tools that need to be in place to support the competencies' development.

CHANGING THE ENVIRONMENT

Bette Manchester described a project, now in its sixth year, "about putting tools in the hands of teachers and students throughout Maine with the vision of economic and workforce development." As a result, all middle school students and teachers now have laptops, software, e-mail, and other resources for collaboration, she reported, and the project has moved into one-third of the state's high schools.

"But it isn't enough just to put technology into the schools," Manchester said. "It really is about changing the 'workplace' there and changing the schools—although giving people technology does help to begin altering what happens in classrooms." In the past, teachers shared a computer lab and had to schedule time to use it. But "if there was a fire drill or the Internet service went down," she said, "you could wait another month or two before the students had that opportunity again." Now, with the agenda pushed into the regular classroom, kids no longer need to go elsewhere and work in isolation.

Integral to changing the schools' environments, and a large part of the project, has been ongoing professional development aided by leadership teams composed of teachers, administrators, and librarians, said Manchester. Their specific goals have been "equity of resources for students and teachers; increasing student and teacher learning; increasing student and teacher collaboration; and increasing project-based and applied learning opportunities in the schools."

To reach these goals, she said, it is important not only for teachers but also for students to have a voice in the management of change. Thus, the project has established student "tech teams" in every school to help ensure students' ability to contribute.

Regarding students' all-important ability to learn, "assessment has been a huge piece for us in how we have them use these tools and show evidence of their learning," Manchester said. "Assessment informs teachers and students about the *next* learning that needs to be taking place in the classroom." Moreover, the project intends that the intellectual capabilities comprising ICT fluency be taught in all classes, not just the high-level ones, "so that all students are actually getting high-level content, rigorous context, and integration of fluency skills."

The project intends that much of this work be based on student projects, some of which occur outside the schools and are therefore informal. According to Manchester, the schools are deeply involved in, and students participate in, a variety of initiatives with colleges, research centers, museums, and community agencies, among others.

She cited some of the state project's challenges that remain: continued funding so that the effort may move forward; flattening the information network in order to provide resources directly to principals, teachers, and students; and local control (as opposed to a state-mandated program). "Maine is a local-control state," said Manchester, "so it is critical that we develop policies and practices that really are much more systemic if we ever are going to get these skills into the schools."

CULTIVATING LIFELONG INTERDEPENDENT LEARNING

Vera Michalchik indicated that while survey organizations have long reported that young people are getting more access to ICT and spending more time with it, we also know that some of them have very limited experience: 15 percent of them do not have access to the Internet at all, she said. In other words, their ICT experience varies greatly.

She went on to say that the question of what youth are doing with ICT depends on who the kids are: it is a function of their gender, disposition, education, and economic situation. In other words, technology is not something that is adopted in any universal sort of way. Its presence and use are reflective of particular social contexts as well as constructed by those social contexts.

When you talk about social context, Michalchik continued, you are talking about relationships. ICT fluency is really a mediated process, a process of learning from others and adapting accordingly. People draw on the competencies of those around them—in community technology centers, in after-school settings, and in informal conversations with friends.

In that sense, the emphasis in *Being Fluent* on independent learning might well be adjusted, she suggested, to capture the social dimensions of ICT. Although the report does discuss collaboration, it talks largely about working *with* other people, not learning *from* other people. "Kids who are sophisticated users become that way in large part by cultivating and adapting their personal relationships," said Michalchik. And they rely not only on "knowledge brokers"—well-informed people, often contemporaries, who they can draw from—but also on "process brokers," such as teachers, who can help them manage the relationships and other resources they need. As an example, Michalchik referred to Phillip Bell's paper for the workshop. It included an example of coders who, as they go through their programming exercises, have established norms within their group that require them to share insights—typically, by blogging on a regular basis—about the code that they are writing.

Therefore, instead of talking about producing lifelong independent learners, she suggested, we should emphasize becoming lifelong *interdependent* learners—often, in informal environments. This would help people escape the "epistemological rut we've been in for over 100 years" that posits legitimate learning as occurring when people are isolated from each other.

Michalchik connected learning through relationships to a particular aspect of assessment. "For many years I have observed that people in social and cultural interaction are constantly assessing what others know because they need to draw on one another's competencies." This is especially what kids do, she said. "They pay attention to what other people know how to do, which is how they learn from the time they are infants. They orient themselves to what other people's capabilities and knowledge are, and they do this seamlessly." Such "embedded interactional assessment," she added, "doesn't just help learning. It also helps people organize their goals as they get together; and it helps them regulate participation in activities, based on who knows how to do what."

Ultimately, Michalchik concluded, "it's about teaching as well, because good teachers are always paying attention, in very subtle interactional ways, to what their students know and know how to do."

MAJOR THEMES

Joyce Malyn-Smith enumerated three of the workshop contributors' major points so far, made both through oral presentations and papers: (1) the need to build foundations for workers of the future; (2) the importance of informal learning as a complement to learning in the schools; and (3) the kinds of things that must be put in a framework: self-direction, interpersonal skills, accountability, adaptability, and social responsibility.

Students need to know how to make sense of information—to extract useful information and identify disinformation, Malyn-Smith observed. They should be sensitive to context, rigor, and relevance. They should develop ICT fluency through blended learning environments: face to face and on line, authentic contexts, apprenticeships, internships, and service learning.

As guidance to teachers in helping students become fluent, she offered an analogy: "When Phil Esposito was asked why he was such a successful hockey player, he said 'It's because I don't skate to where the puck is. I skate to where it's going to go.'" Similarly, Malyn-Smith suggested, "as we think about fluency, we need to consider where it's going to be in a few years and structure what we can do to get us there." Highlighting another important suggestion, she noted that implementation of ICT fluency—unlike the original report's vision of a unique course designed and offered in the school—should be embedded throughout the curriculum. "The end goal of being fluent," she said, "is not just to use the tools but to use them to help you learn English or help you learn science."

Philip Sumida observed that embeddedness cuts both ways. Citing another workshop participant, he said that "the question becomes how we identify the characteristics in institutions that will make them change their focus from 'I'm teaching Chaucer' to 'I'm teaching ambiguity and change.'"

He also emphasized that with respect to teaching skills such as networking, teachers are not the critical link. "Students are learning networking themselves. They will go and find each other, whether it's on their mobile phones, instant messaging, or whatever it is. And they are very good at this. But while they don't need us to teach them how to network, they do need us to teach them how to use these networks successfully to accomplish the sorts of goals of their workplaces."

Regarding how to change institutions in order to achieve such outcomes, Sumida acknowledged that "there is no one right way." Nevertheless, he added, "we can identify the characteristics of those institutions that make them more *likely* to have students who meet fluency goals."

WHAT SCHOOLS SHOULD LOOK LIKE

In response to several questions from the audience about elements of the Maine project's success, as well as any notable difficulties, Manchester first credited individuals outside the K–12 teaching arena. "It actually took the vision of a governor who put his whole career on the line," she said, "and we spent a fair amount of time with Seymour Papert [an eminent computer scientist and educator], so we got the vision right."

But ultimately, she said, the project succeeded by "taking best-practice people and putting them in the driver's seat." Content area by content area, she said, the project employs a "distinguished educator line" to secure the most qualified individuals to guide their colleagues. For example, "in the area of science I pulled a science teacher who ran our base college academies for math and science, and he is working with the science teachers to embed resources and tools into their work." The project did the same for literacy teachers and for arts. "These people are working with teachers around the state," she said.

Success in any given school, however, depends in large part on the quality of its leadership team, Manchester said. And remarkably, she has observed a strong inverse correlation between such leadership quality, or the relative lack of it, and a pedestrian but easy-to-document measure—the school's record of equipment breakage. Such data are of course anecdotal, she acknowledged, but "schools that have less damage are usually doing really interesting and exciting things. You walk into the school, and you feel it. You spend time with the teachers and the leadership team, and you see a real problem-solving organization, where people are taking risks, analyzing what they are doing, then going back again and trying something different. And that is directly related to the kinds of interesting and exciting things going on for kids in the classroom."

By contrast, she noted, "when I go to a school that has high breakage, it takes me five minutes to see that there is no leadership team. There is no purpose of the work. There is no vision for the work. And the tech coordinator and principal are often at odds, with the tech coordinator actually in charge of the building when it comes to IT."

This observation highlights a continuing problem in the project, Manchester said. "We still have way too many administrators abdicating their role as educational leader to the tech people, who decide, for example, whether a school will have e-mail." Compounding the problem is that information from national programs tends to get sent to the tech people, not to school principals. State by state, she observed, we need to turn such situations around.

Cullinane was asked a comparable question regarding Microsoft's School of the Future Project: In being "continuous, relevant, and adaptive," what will such schools look like? By definition, *continuous* implies independence of time and place, she responded. "So our strategies clearly involve a wireless infrastructure, on-line resources, all materials being digital, and students having one-to-one access." There should also be a continuum in access, with school and home having similar access to online environments. Broadband access at school, for instance, should mean broadband access at home—admittedly a challenge in West Philadelphia.

Relevant, she continued, refers to instruction, which means that teachers and students have access to up-to-date materials and up-to-date tools. And *adaptive* "means an environment in which students have the ability to drive their own learning—that is, to use self-directed learning models where individuals can, based on where they are, go the way they need to go—as opposed to 'Do I have to go the way the student next to me needs to go?'"

Meanwhile, delivery of individualized assessments, in real time to a student's desktop, will be technologically enabled by "virtual teaching assistants," Cullinane said. "Students will then be pointed in a specific direction. If they need remediation on the topic, they will be directed to digital materials that support the remediation. If they can go further, they will be pointed toward resources that serve that purpose."

Asked about useful analogs for helping educators effect the kind of broad organizational changes that such innovations imply, Cullinane referred to a seemingly universal characteristic of successful organizations. "At the end of the day, it comes down to the fact that they consist of people who, without question, have the attitude of 'I want to be better.' If you look at companies that are successful, if you look at teams that are successful, their people are passionate about the idea of 'I'm going to own that, I'm going to be responsible for it.' That's the environment we are trying to create in this [School of the Future], and if we can do it there we hope to have a model that can be replicated worldwide."

Malyn-Smith pointed out that an essential aspect of such environments is a culture that encourages creative thinking and risk taking, neither of which is typical of education systems. Similarly, although it is essential to give teachers the tools that everyone else has in the workplace, resources are so limited that they often compromise the goal of ICT fluency. "It is unacceptable," she said, "for a science teacher to stand up and say 'I don't have Internet access, and I have one computer in my classroom.' How do you expect them to turn things around?"

"We are a long way from some of the things that we have been talking about today," Cullinane acknowledged. "But we have two choices. We can conclude that the issue is so huge that it's simply overwhelming. Or we can bite off a small piece of the issue, try to address that, and hope that what we learn from it can be modeled and scaled nationwide. At Microsoft we are taking the latter of those two approaches."

PARENTAL INVOLVEMENT

Session chair Herb Lin, of the National Academies' Computer Science and Telecommunications Board, noted that "one of the things I've seen in trying to promote educational change at the precollege level is the resistance of parents to things that are different." So given what Cullinane and Manchester "are trying to do in a new, adaptive, dynamic, student-centered, inquiry-oriented, educational environment, which is very different from the ones that most parents had when they were students," Lin asked, had the speakers encountered any parental resistance?

Cullinane said that she and her colleagues had not experienced such resistance, and she attributed its absence to the disadvantaged nature of the neighborhood, West Philadelphia, which she equated to East Harlem. "These parents are so hopeful for this opportunity for their students," Cullinane said, "that they couldn't jump on board faster." In fact, she reported, parents have often helped to restore the School of the Future team's occasionally sagging morale. Just by calling a community meeting, "the folks can come and build us all back up," she said. "It's a shot of inspiration." Cullinane speculated, on whether resistance is a function of parents' level of education and degree of financial success. That might be the basis of a good study, she suggested.

Manchester said that her experience supports this hypothesis. "We haven't seen any resistance from parents who've lost their jobs in the manufacturing world and really want to see their kids learn and have a different life," she said. By contrast, resistance to doing our kind of large-scale project has come from among "the best-educated we have in Maine"— people who have been some of the most vocal as well. For example, she noted that with the Laptop Project, parents were initially quite concerned about giving an expensive tool to children that they wouldn't take care of, though it turned out that they did.

Cullinane said that educators' emphasis on technology per se, especially in their interactions with parents, ought to stop. "If we can talk about the environment that needs to be created so that we can improve student achievement, as well as student preparation for what will lie beyond, we don't even have to mention the word 'technology.' But if we keep going back to hardware or machines or software or typing skills in our conversation with parents, we are going to get bogged down in the weeds." Of course, she acknowledged, we cannot get where we want to go without technology. "But if we talk about an involved and interconnected learning community, we don't have to argue the value of technology because the end goal is understood."

Manchester agreed that while dropping reference to technology is desirable in theory, it is not always possible in practice, especially when state legislators and local boards must make decisions about funding new technology for the schools or staying with textbooks—that is, whether to move ahead or risk falling behind. "For us right now," she said, "we are still at the level of needing the support to survive in the kind of environment we have created for schools."

6

Assessments to
Measure Students' Competencies

- *How can one measure high school students' skills, capabilities, and grasp of concepts with respect to information and communications technology (ICT)?*
- *What assessment tools exist or are under development?*
- *What are the challenges of developing large-scale assessments of ICT fluency?*

Following the two sessions devoted to exploring the kinds of outcomes needed and specific strategies and approaches for achieving them, this session essentially addressed the measurement of outcomes. Its aim was to acquaint workshop participants with creative practices and tools that have been developed to assess students' ICT competencies.

Speakers described a variety of assessment vehicles aimed at diverse ages, ranging from relatively narrow applications up to "high-stakes" tests administered on a national scale. Presenters suggested, however, that the underlying principles were generalizable, with the principal differences among tests being degree of difficulty. In other words, innovative ICT tests for college students or professional license applicants could, with relatively modest intellectual adjustment, be useful in designing assessments for high school students as well. One speaker also described an ambitious national program of assessments designed directly for K–12 students.

Presenters were Martin Ripley, head of e-strategy at the Qualification Curriculum Authority (QCA) of the United Kingdom; Irvin Katz, a senior research scientist at the Educational Testing Service's Center for Assessment, Innovation, and Technology Transfer; and John Behrens, senior manager of assessment development and innovation at Cisco Systems.

INNOVATION AND EXCITEMENT IN THE UNITED KINGDOM

Noting that QCA is the government body responsible for the U.K.'s curricula, standards, examinations, and assessments for all students ages 5–16, Martin Ripley spoke in particular about the national curriculum's "Key Stage 3," which covers students in grades 7–9 (ages 11–14). He said that while the testing of these students in the subjects of English, mathematics, and science has been compulsory since 1994, the agency plans to add four new statutory tests—in ICT—in 2008. These tests are high stakes, Ripley said. "The results are published on a school-by-school basis by the national government, and because they are made available to every parent and every school governor in the country, these results are used for school accountability purposes."

The ICT curriculum for Key Stage 3, he said, has four basic components:

1. Finding things out—a student's ability to select an appropriate source and assess the value of the information thus obtained.
2. Developing ideas and making things happen—for example, using ICT to measure, record, respond to, and control events.
3. Exchanging and sharing information—using ICT for such purposes as Web publishing or video conferencing.
4. Reviewing, modifying, and evaluating work as it progresses.

QCA has set increasingly stringent standards, ranging from level 1 to level 8, on what students are expected to achieve as they progress through their schooling. Ripley said that a 13-year-old should be achieving level 5, which includes such abilities as creating sequences of instructions to control events and exploring the effects of changing the variables in ICT models, among numerous other skills.

Ripley described the elements of testing that ascertain whether or not the curriculum is yielding student performance at the desired standard levels. Tests are designed, he said, to articulate nine ICT capabilities:

1. Searching and selecting—"an aspect of finding things out."
2. Organizing and structuring—"using systemic approaches to find-

ing things out."

3. Developing ideas—"students' ability to measure and record."
4. Exchanging information—"primarily communication."
5. Reviewing—"for the purposes of improvement."
6. Defining tasks—"students' ability to characterize the tasks that they are being asked to complete."
7. Control—"using technology to make things happen."
8. Modeling—"using ICT as a tool.
9. Presenting information—"using forms of technology for the purposes of presentation."

Ripley briefly summarized key components of his current project. Regarding the first component—getting the schools' infrastructure ready—he noted that there had been an investment to ensure access to computers and broadband.

In describing the actual test program and the kinds of questions posed, Ripley showed several screen graphs of Key Stage 3 ICT tasks that are presented to children. These tests "are a virtual world we have created that mimics very closely a Windows-based desktop environment," he said. Entirely within its confines—i.e., not through the Internet—students log on to a test section and have access to a variety of applications built for the purposes of that test. Behind an *intra*net Web browser, for example, "sits a whole plethora of different Websites, on different resources and kinds of information, that the student can gain access to" for use in addressing a given task. The designed tasks are typically presented to students in an e-mail message to their screens.

For example, one task may ask them to go into the virtual world in order to update a hotel leaflet aimed at attracting more guests. This particular task, Ripley noted, is "reasonably scaffolded. It provides instructions and directions, making clear to students that the leaflet needs to be updated, that it needs a photo of the swimming pool, that the prices should be inserted, and even that they should save their work." Scoring this task, he said "is a matter of electronically eavesdropping on how children set about solving the task—whether students use keyboard shortcuts in order to navigate around the virtual world we have created, how they select the photograph, whether they check the validity of the information on prices."

Another example, less scaffolded, is a partly finished presentation for display in a shopping center. Students are provided with a number of comments on the presentation from different sources, and they are asked to update it in light of those comments. "In this case we are looking for higher-order thinking from the students," said Ripley. "We are asking them to make judgments about the comments and to engage in quite a sustained activity—of 15 or maybe 20 minutes—to complete the presentation." As in the preceding example, and for all other tasks, students are scored against the nine ICT capabilities.

"What we have created is truly innovative, exciting, and robust," Ripley said. But he acknowledged that "at the moment it is 'wrong footing' many teachers and many students." For example, in a pilot version of this type of test involving 45,000 students, which QCA ran during the summer of 2005, it was evident that "students are really very unfamiliar with this mode of taking a test and that lack of familiarity clearly impacted on student performance." Many students ran out of time, encountered technical difficulties, or showed underdeveloped technique. The bottom line, he said, is that they had weaknesses in two main areas: modeling and data handling.

Meanwhile, Ripley observed, "there is some depth of concern that ICT performance in our schools has not been as close to the mark as we would like it to be—students' achievement is good or better in only 54 percent of lessons, and with huge variation from school to school. Though ICT performance continues to improve, it's still the subject where there is the most underachievement in schools."

The country's goals are ambitious, however. "A team of about 400 people nationally has responsibility to get 85 percent of our students to reach the level 5 target by 2007," he said. In pursuit of that objective, the team is focusing especially on the preparation of teachers.

A VIEW FROM THE EDUCATIONAL TESTING SERVICE

Irvin Katz pointed out that his extensive involvement in ICT skills assessment pertained to ICT literacy, rather than ICT fluency, which was the focus of the workshop. But he suggested that ICT literacy—which he and his colleagues at the Educational Testing Service (ETS) have formally defined as the "ability to use digital technologies, communication tools, and/or networks to access, manage, integrate, evaluate, create, and communicate information ethically and legally in order to function in a knowledge society"—is just a particular subset of ICT fluency. It is basically "information literacy as it is viewed through the use of technology," Katz said.

He also noted that while his work has been geared to higher education, the kinds of assessments that he and his colleagues have developed are readily transferable, and in both directions: to precollege (K–12) systems; and beyond college, to graduate schools and workplaces. The differences between these assessment levels, he said, would largely be a matter of difficulty.

ETS's overall model of ICT literacy has seven components, which are aligned with the standards of the American Council of Research Libraries:

1. Define an information need.
2. Access resources and information.
3. Manage information.
4. Integrate information through interpretation and synthesis.
5. Evaluate resources and information.
6. Create new information or adapt existing information.
7. Communicate information to particular audiences.

Katz stressed that these components emphasize cognitive skills—intellectual capabilities—rather than the technical skills involved in using particular technologies. For example, students may be presented with a half-completed spreadsheet, given a little time to accommodate themselves to that type of spreadsheet, and then be asked to complete it using the resources they have been given. The components also address ethical issues, he said, such as knowledge about citations or the ability to deal effectively with confidential information.

ETS's testing of these skills has been framed around modest scenarios aimed at "simulating real-world types of activities," Katz said. "We have taken this big, sustained type of reasoning and broken it up into little pieces. We provide all the information that students would need at that point, and they take it the next step." He noted as well that this approach "allows us to collect a lot of data on each individual in a relatively short amount of time."

The current version of the test, Katz reported, is delivered over the Internet and is 75 minutes long. It consists of 14 short tasks, each of which targets one or more components of the ICT literacy model. There is also a longer, 15-minute task that targets two of the skills and starts to look at integration across skills.

He offered several examples, speaking at length on a task "designed to target integration: taking information from a bunch of places, summarizing it, and then drawing some type of conclusion from that summary." The problem asks students to imagine that they work at an architecture firm that happens to employ a lot of left-handed people and that the boss

wants to find some vendors of left-handed products. Information (in vary-
ing degrees of explicitness) on three vendors is provided in three different
electronic formats, and students must decide how to extract the specific
information needed and then how to compare the products from those
different vendors. Finally, students have to rank the vendors and provide a
recommendation.

In keeping with the purpose of assessing students' intellectual capabilities, they are scored on how well they figure out what it is they need to
compare, how well they pull that information from the available resources,
and how well they draw conclusions. Scoring other tasks might involve, for
example, how well students search the Internet or a database, critically
evaluate information, decide on what resources are more authoritative, or
develop presentations that meet some main objective. In the latter case,
Katz said, "key aspects include: Are you meeting the information needs of
your audience? And are you supporting whatever main point it is that you
want to make?"

Feedback about test performance "is not so much detailed scores," he
said, because those wouldn't be very reliable. Rather, feedback largely consists of a discussion of the types of strengths and weaknesses that the student has shown, together with some recommendations on the types of tasks
he or she might do, working with an instructor, to improve."

Katz concluded by citing five benefits of such assessments of ICT
literacy:

1. Supporting institutional ICT-literacy initiatives.
2. Guiding curricular innovations and evaluating curricular changes.
3. Guiding individual learning.
4. Providing a "stake in the ground" for what ICT skills look like.
5. Providing a model for teachers of possible assignments.

BROAD AND NARROW ASSESSMENT

John Behrens noted that because the word "assessment" has different
meanings for different people, it is important to make clear what one
is referring to under any given set of circumstances. For example, he
asked, "Are we talking instructional, formative, summative, or diagnostic
assessment?"

Behrens said that in his work at the Cisco Networking Academy, the

Cisco Professional Certification Program, and Cisco University, a construct called the Seven Cs—claims, curriculum, collaboration, complexity, computation, communication, and coordination (plus an eighth: contextualization)—defines assessment of outcomes from training programs involving the company's products and services.

Behrens cited as well a useful delivery model, called evidence-centered design, that has four basic parts: task selection, presentation, evidence observation, and evidence accumulation. In other words, he said, the assessment cycle is "interact, look at what you've got back, characterize it, and decide what to do next."

Out of Cisco's vast curriculum- and assessment-design work, both internal and external—it has partnered with over 10,000 schools in 150 countries, Behrens said—he offered a variety of examples ranging from pilot projects for testing students to simulation tasks used in professional certification exams. Discussing simulations at some length, he described their basic language at Cisco (Internetworking Operating System), their applications, and the ways in which their results can be presented.

Behrens stressed the utility of a digital format for providing diverse types of feedback both to instructors and students. It can place item-level information into a grade book, for instance, and provide verbal feedback together with scoring rules, he said. Instructors are also given the work products and user logs so that they can score the test themselves, if they wish, or look for other patterns.

"A great thing going on in the world right now, which we are all excited about, is the integration of instruction and assessment," Behrens said. He described a tool, made available to instructors without charge on the Internet, called Packet Tracer. "It allows students of digital networking systems—by themselves or in groups—to practice planning, design, or troubleshooting," he said. "And it can be used for assessment, both formally and informally, in class and out of class." Such an approach, Behrens maintained, is clearly the wave of the future. "Because the world is becoming more digital, the aids for describing the world are becoming more digital too," he said. "Assessment people need to use these tools rather than reinvent the wheel every time."

Eric Klopfer, director of the Teacher Education Program at the Massachusetts Institute of Technology, raised the issue of potential bias in the presentation of such digitally based assessments to students. In assigning tasks by email, for example, some students, depending on the e-mail applications that they customarily use, if any, might be disadvantaged, he said.

Ripley admitted that he and his colleagues in the United Kingdom often feel torn between offering a "reductionist" test (presenting a task so that virtually all students will be familiar with it) and elevating the test (trying to raise the minimum expectation for students). Because his agency's mission is to design "high-stakes" assessments that offer "a very similar test experience for all students" around the country, it is important to try to minimize any bias in such environments.

Similarly, Katz pointed out that ETS—in using e-mail, for example, in its testing—"tries to come up with something generic" that will likely resemble whatever a student is used to. Moreover, in echoing a major point from his talk, he noted that "we are focusing not so much on the technology but on what people are doing with the information that is presented." Still, he acknowledged, "it is hard to avoid some aspect of bias."

Ripley added that administration of tests in a digital environment might actually *reduce* bias. QCA wanted to know "which students, in which categories of need, we would exclude if we went down a digital front—a screen route—for formulating tasks." So it did a study, completed in 2004, "Our top-line conclusion was that we were enabling more students to access the tasks on screen than if they were on paper," said Ripley. "So we are certainly not doing more harm than in paper-based tests. And I would argue that we are facilitating engagement, not preventing engagement, with the test."

Heidi Schweingruber of the National Academies' Board on Science Education raised the issue of ICT embeddedness in content areas—an often-mentioned idea during the workshop—and noted that it did not seem to be reflected in the discussion of assessments. Ripley acknowledged that so far "this has been a challenge for us. Our tests look rather like standardized ICT lessons, or business applications of ICT, and not even school-based applications of ICT." But the omission has been noted, he said, and about two years ago his agency began development work in this area. Colleagues are making progress, he suggested, though "the material is not yet ready to show publicly or to use in any of our test administrations."

7

Revisiting the *Being Fluent* Framework

In the first part of this session, a panel of experts—authors of the workshop's papers and an author's representative—discussed the papers and their implications. In the second part of the session, the workshop participants met in seven small groups to discuss two assigned questions. Their responses, the organizing committee expected, would provide "actionable items" for updating the *Being Fluent* framework and, ultimately, for measuring its success in cultivating information and communications technology (ICT) fluency in high school students. The final part of the session was devoted to reports from the breakout groups.

EXPERTS' REFLECTIONS

Useful Social Practices

Philip Bell a member of the Board on Science Education at the National Research Council began this session. He said that in rereading *Being Fluent*'s 30 characteristics of "FITness" (fluency with information technology) he noted some resonance with general aspects of problem solving. He also saw in those characteristics a tension between two poles: a "designer or builder view" and a "sophisticated-user view." The latter, he said, being more tightly coupled to personal objectives, affects the use of information technologies on a day-to-day basis. Thus "there is much to be gained by actually understanding some of these sophisticated everyday uses of ICT," Bell said, and he pointed to studies that he and his colleagues are doing with respect to children's ICT activities in and out of school.

The researchers are observing several on-line spaces where kids, out of school, spend a good deal of time talking with each other about various topics—particularly those that are personally consequential, such as having to do with their understanding of health and their making of health-related decisions. "We are looking at the kinds of argumentation they do in those settings and how those particular technologies allow them to have particular kinds of discussions around data or ideas," said Bell.

The in-school part of his work has been around scaffolding students' engagement with scientific evidence. The researchers are trying to see what kinds of supports kids need in order to acquire disciplinary understandings of information they find on the Internet and to create meaningful arguments from that information.

Bell and his colleagues have also been spending time, he said, "following the trends of technology and popular culture. There we are seeing quite a bit of integrated, really tightly bound-up use of ICT in children's everyday activities across all sorts of settings." So, for example, with participants who are available on their "instant messenger" list 15 hours a day, "we are trying to understand how that shapes their experience differently from children who are not in that kind of contact with a distributed network of close peers."

Bell explained that there are two parts to this investigation. The first is focused on cognition and learning with the aid of ICT. Research in this area explores the degree to which learning is domain-specific or domain-general, how people navigate the Internet for information, and how the cognitive work that people do crosses different contexts and domains. The second part focuses on social practices, which he argued are very useful in ICT education activities because they help engage students in a much more concrete way. Bell has observed, for example, that in communities whose members have shared norms about how they cultivate information and share it with each other, individuals are socially obligated to be contributing valuable information to that community as much as they are taking information away. Such "very fit social practices" serve both the group and its individual members.

Authentic Contexts

Paul Resta pointed out the need to be attentive to pedagogical challenges. *Being Fluent*, for example, maintained that, while lecturing is not the most powerful mode or even an effective mode for helping students develop ICT fluency, project-based learning could be a major asset. "We need to be providing a more authentic context for learning ICT fluency," he said. "Students learn best when they are engaged in authentic tasks and using authentic technological tools. We really need to create those environments." Resta thus agreed with other participants' suggestions to make schools more like workplaces, and he would go even further. "A critical step toward making that happen is to formally connect the school with the workplace. We can look at service learning programs, apprenticeships, and internships," he said, "and I think this is particularly important for low-income minority students."

Resta noted his work with Native American school communities. "If you can engage those students in tasks that are meaningful both to them personally and to their community," he said, "it is a powerful tool for helping to direct ICT fluency." In his center's Four Directions Project, for example, students not only become technology experts in such settings but also act as partners with teachers and elders in helping to develop culturally responsive curricula.

Meanwhile, Resta said, *teacher* education is critical. Colleges must not only prepare teachers with the skills they will need to foster ICT fluency but should also ensure that all graduates have been on the same page with respect to platforms, software, and basic approaches to creating fruitful environments for their students.

Unpredictable Effects

Paul Horwitz commented on the difficulty of predicting the future—how we tend to "get the innovation right but don't realize what effect it's going to have." So, for example, when the telephone was invented some 125 years ago, it was seen as a better interface for the telegraph. The automobile was thought to be like a horse, only faster, and the printing press was merely a way to reduce the cost of books. Each of these technologies achieved those specific ends, he said, but they also went much further. Indeed, he suggested, they revolutionized the world.

Similarly, while Benjamin Franklin invented the public library so that everyone could have access to information, we now have it a lot faster, Horwitz said. "Nonlinearities happen when you make information available that much faster, when you no longer have to go to the library and look something up in a book." Thus, *Being Fluent*, published in 1999, couldn't possibly imagine, for example, the rise of blogs, he said. "Everybody can publish now, and the amazing thing is that people read them." Another example is Webcams, whereby people give up their privacy, on purpose, so that others can watch them over the course of their regular day. Horwitz said, "There is a phenomenon here of the global village that is qualitatively different from what was going on before."

Not only are the effects of an innovation a lot greater than one would think, he noted, they are both good and bad. While the car has introduced a great many benefits to the world, it is also the leading cause of death of young people. And while useful information is available on the Internet, a lot of what is there may be useless or even harmful. For example, "it's now very easy for rumors to get around very quickly and to be believed by a very large number of people without regard to whether they have any relation to the truth," said Horwitz.

"The key questions," he concluded are, "What is the responsibility of the school to head off such problems?" and "What is the responsibility of society in general?"

Rules of Engagement

Vivian Guilfoy, senior vice president for Education, Employment, and Community Programs at the Education Development Center, represented author Karen Pittman, who was unable to attend.

An important point made in the Pittman paper, Guilfoy said, is that "huge numbers of our young people are not in school. They are in homeless shelters, community-based agencies, facilities of the Department of Justice, or in jobs—sometimes good jobs, sometimes horrible jobs." It is imperative, she said, that we reach them and work with them.

A second point of the paper is that a great deal of ICT activity is occurring outside school in the "informal" sector. For example, Guilfoy said, "community-based organizations have for quite a long time been doing incredible work in ICT." Volunteers from the business sector often are passionately involved, making valuable resources available. "We should be asking ourselves," she said, "how we can improve and leverage the kinds of activities that these people do in order to reach the FITness goals and protocols we have been talking about?"

And a third point of Pittman's paper is to be very careful with "laundry lists," Guilfoy said. We can't just check off the three designations of the *Being Fluent* framework but must establish hierarchies among components and show how they relate to each other.

At the heart of all this, she said, "is something called engagement: How do we hook our young people, as well as those who are working with our young people, to get interested? And, whether the motivation is to get a job, answer a question they really care about, or to do good for somebody else, I think we underestimate what some of the motivators might be for our young people."

One important avenue for educators of FITness, she noted, is to show students how different sectors, different disciplines, and policy makers and practitioners alike can come together to achieve successful results. "We need to think as creatively as we can about how to honestly learn from one another," said Guilfoy. "How can we make sure that we are talking about things that 'say yes?'" Rather than stereotyping and compartmentalizing would-be participants, she said, the attitude should be "yes, we can do this together; and yes, we can find innovative ways to make this happen."

PARTICIPANTS' VIEWS

In the breakout sessions, participants were asked to consider two questions:

1. Listening and participating in the conversations at this meeting, as well as drawing from your own experiences, what revisions would you recommend to the ICT fluency framework offered in *Being Fluent with Information Technology?*
2. How would you know when this framework has been implemented well in the context of high schools?

In the final plenary session, when each group reported on its responses to the questions, every group leader qualified his or her remarks in much the same way. A summary of the group's discussion, they said, would miss the nuanced flavor of participants' comments. Yet they agreed that their summaries would capture the main points of the discussions. Although there was considerable overlap among the groups in these main points, there also were notable differences.

The rest of this section covers that final session in the order of the questions.

Should the *Being Fluent* Framework Be Revised?

The groups discussed both the overall framework and its three areas: intellectual capabilities, foundational concepts, and contemporary skills.

Overall Framework

There was some agreement that the fluency framework (see Box 2-1 in Chapter 2) can be moved from the college level to high school, with minor revisions in each of its three areas. However, one group noted that the language used in the framework is often not clear enough for potential supporters, such as policy makers, to stand behind. For example, under intellectual capabilities, component 10 ("Think about information technology abstractly") is itself too abstract. Thus there is a need to be more concrete. In this vein, another group suggested that a revision of *Being Fluent*, or perhaps a secondary document, should have examples specific to disciplines and provide some vision and practical suggestions to teachers. Yet another group noted that because many of the information technology concepts are related to each other, they might be more effectively described at the meta level.

Two of the groups suggested that the framework be seriously revisited so that its components are made measurable in assessment-friendly ways. One group suggested that a single unified framework, in place of the three discrete areas, would be better. The other group observed that the notion of "generating useful content," which is certainly essential to ICT fluency, is a straightforward process for students made unnecessarily complex by the framework: to describe that notion, one needs to invoke a skill, a concept, and a capability.

An issue that the *Being Fluent* report is silent about is the need to provide a legal and safe operating environment for students. Just as everyone wants to make sure that students don't have guns in school, an atmosphere must be established there that lets students pursue their intellectual activities lawfully. Similarly, there should be some guidance on mobilizing and organizing.

Intellectual Capabilities

One group suggested that "collaborate" (component 6) be modified to "interact with others" at the high school level. This group also said that "think about information technology abstractly" (component 10) may be less complicated at the secondary level than at the college level, while another group recommended that this component be filled out by extending it or complementing it with something on the order of "think about practical applications." One group noted that a missing idea in the framework is "creativity," though it is not clear how to specify such a component.

There were two suggestions for merging components. One was to merge "test a solution" (component 3) and "manage problems in faulty solutions" (component 4). The other was to merge "expect the unexpected" (component 8) and "anticipate changing technologies" (component 9) into something like "anticipate and adapt changing technologies to changing situations." This formulation would lead to recognition, which could ultimately lead to a response. Another group suggested that one component should be expanded: "create information" should be added to "organize and navigate information structures and evaluate information" (component 5).

Finally, one group expressed some concern about "ontological muddling"—components at different levels of abstraction. At the very least, there needs to be more detail about what the components mean.

Foundational Concepts

One group noted that as the ICT world has changed since *Being Fluent* was published, some of the components and terms in the framework need to change too. For example, components 1 and 3, "computers" and "networks," should be collapsed, as they are collapsing in industry. When computers are no longer stand-alone devices but elements of distributed systems, what is a network and what is a computer?

Several groups proposed additions to this area of the framework. One group offered "pervasive and ubiquitous computing" and another said "computational science" should be included in component 8. Another group said that issues of security, privacy, and ethics should be included. Also offered for inclusion was the issue of participating in communities, though the group that offered it said it is unclear whether it ought to be under concepts or skills.

Contemporary Skills

The group discussions about this area of the framework covered both overall ideas and specific changes. One group noted that while the collections of components under intellectual capabilities and foundational concepts will largely hold their own over time, a mechanism needs to be in place for updating the components of ICT skills on a periodic basis. Another group observed that some of the ICT skills aim too low, applying in large measure to current elementary school students. These skills should be elevated for the high school level.

More specifically, several groups suggested altering terms to reflect changes in the ICT environment. One proposal was to change "graphic" to "interactive media" in component 4 ("using a graphic and/or artwork package to create illustrations, slides, or other image-based expressions of ideas"). Another proposal was to change "a computer" to "digital devices" in component 7 ("using a computer to communicate with others").

One group proposed a complete rewording of component 3: from "using a word processor to create a text document" to "using application software to create useful documents." Another group said that component 10 ("using instructional materials to learn how to use new applications or features") needs to be broadened, as instructional materials are not always satisfactory. When revised, this item might refer, for example, to the kinds of technologies, systems, or general processes that students should look for. Lastly, one group suggested that there should be a component about being able to secure one's computer.

How Can ICT Fluency Be Assessed or Measured?

Agreeing with the *Being Fluent* report that an effective way to integrate the different kinds of ICT-related knowledge is to be involved in projects— which are realistic instances of ICT application in daily life—one group focused on ways to judge students' contributions. It suggested that students would have to create "artifacts" from their work that could be evaluated. Such evaluations would not be based on how many buttons the item has or on some other quantitative measure, but would be done in the way in which, for example, art is judged by a jury and books are reviewed. Given that such artifacts would be much more complex than students' traditional products, they would be worthy of much more complex evaluation.

Another possibility, assuming that ICT has been embedded across all high school learning experience, would be *not* to evaluate ICT fluency per se. In this approach, students would not be expected to achieve fluency through a single class; rather, they would become fluent through exposure in all of their classes. For example, students would learn some components in physics, some in history, and some in writing.

Another group talked about shared libraries of projects and plans, such as the Digital Library of Earth Science Education, that people would be able to sort through for ideas for lessons. The elements of such resources could be categorized by the degree to which they relate to ICT fluency. At the same time, the fluency framework as a whole could be used in science, technology, engineering, and mathematics (STEM) classes or applied to STEM materials that go beyond the typical content. This group suggested that one might see the framework justified by a research base and well implemented at local and state levels. The accompanying assessments, meanwhile, would have to be well integrated and systematic.

The next group to report noted that because a single evaluation usually gives a misleading impression of what is going on, it is important to have multimodal evaluations—that is, a portfolio of assessments. This led the group to the basic question of whether formal assessments can actually reveal whether students are mastering the material. In graduate school, for example, thesis advisors know very well how their students are doing— what they know and don't know—and they often don't give them an exam at all. So, too, it may be desirable to teach high school teachers how to internalize—to understand, outside a formal structure of testing—the depth of students' knowledge.

In that spirit, the group discussed Bette Manchester's comment (see Chapter 5) that she can go into a school and within minutes feel what is going on there. They would like her to sit her down "with bright lights," they said, "to make her tell us what she knows about the things that evoke those feelings!"

The next group proposed several ways in which success in cultivating ICT fluency among high school students could be measured. One would be if FITness were presented in a less jargon-like way so that everyone could understand it. Another measure of success would be if teachers had to know how to use technology effectively in learning. Another would be if there are buy-ins up and down the "food chain." Success could also be measured if both the students and teachers were moved from being users to being creators—even innovators. And a final measure of success would be if, in assessing kids, the same technology were used that the students are using to learn.

The next group reported that it too had focused on the need for jargon-free presentation and seamless embeddedness. Its discussion emphasized the need for a revised *Being Fluent* or follow-up report to have clear and crisp examples that illustrate what ICT fluency looks like. Group members also talked about the idea of fluency as continuous, relevant, and adaptive: this would provide an interesting way to get a new lens on the kinds of skills and competencies that are needed both in the workplace and higher education. Such an approach would move assessment away from a focus on the usual laundry list.

The next group started from the understanding that ICT literacy would be benchmarked at eighth grade, as required by the No Child Left Behind legislation. As a result, high school would not be a place for acquiring technological literacy skills but rather a place to become fluent with ICT. The group concluded that the focus at the secondary level should be on how you use the technology to learn—how you use it to deepen your knowledge, to work together, and to create. Given that focus, members discussed how to reach classroom teachers: What do we need to see in place to actually get a classroom teacher not only to know about technology but also be able to use it in the classroom?

The group thus proposed several steps that members thought would be useful in achieving these goals:

- It would be important to align or develop a crosswalk of the *Being Fluent* framework with national standards, which are the legacy documents used by states to create the state standards around technology. In that way, there would be an overarching connection of all the things that states are using—such as the 21st Century Skills (see http://www.ncrel.org/engauge/skills/techlit.htm [accessed March 2006]) or the ISTE (International Society for Technology in Education) standards—to drive their own curricula. Alternative strategies for developing skills, such as librarians and teachers collaborating to create lessons for the classroom or to identify big projects that kids could work on together, would also need to be in place.
- There should be an alignment between ICT fluency and content standards as well. In that way, science teachers, for example, would be expected not only to teach youngsters how to develop databases but also to motivate them to analyze subject-related information from the many databases that exist.
- To align the capabilities, concepts, and skills in the *Being Fluent* framework with specific content standards and requirements that

teachers are responsible for, a revised *Being Fluent* or its successor should be more specific. More layers are needed beneath the framework's language for this report to be useful to teachers. In that way, teachers may be able to connect the capabilities, concepts, and skills to the competencies they are responsible for teaching in the classroom and also to be able to integrate ICT fluency into assessment.

- There is a need for dissemination—an intentional plan to reach classroom teachers and provide them with suggestions on how they can use the framework in the classroom.

The final group to report on its discussions offered several examples of assessing outcomes. If remedial ICT programs in community colleges, four-year universities, or companies were to evaporate, they reported, that would be an observable example of success. If there were a universal expectation of a digital portfolio, above and beyond a transcript, for transferring artifacts of work—real products—from the high schools to whatever postsecondary experience people have, that would be another observable example. So too would be the embedding of such expectations into standards, because standards frame the discussion of assessment and professional practice.

Another example: If computer-application classes disappeared because ICT was so fully embedded into real practice, that absence would demonstrate progress. So too would be the embedding of expectations for ICT in the standards that frame the discussion of assessment and professional practice. And if all members of a community, from students to parents to the school-board members to the business people, were using the same vocabulary for conversations like the one we have had over the last two days, that would be a measure of broad ICT fluency.

In closing the workshop, Margaret Honey summarized three critical points that had emerged during the discussions. One was the changing requirements of the workplace and what it means to be successful in the world: very different qualities and skills are required today in comparison with those of previous decades. Second, participants repeatedly emphasized the importance of teaching these skills, notably by embedding them throughout the curriculum. Finally, participants discussed the importance of rigor, relevance, and social context and of the close links between curriculum and assessment. Assessment can be a dynamic and fluid process that is intimately tied to instruction and learning.

Afterword

Jean Moon and Heidi Schweingruber

The Workshop on Information and Communications Technology (ICT) Fluency and High School Graduation Outcomes provided a useful forum for surveying the current status of information and communication technology within the school landscape, charting future directions, and exploring new terrain. Discussions across the day and a half revealed that young people have great interest in ICT but also that educators are not at all clear about the best way to meaningfully bring it into the process of K–12 education. Workshop participants repeatedly stressed that while *Being Fluent* (National Research Council, 1999) was a major step forward in specifying outcomes through its framework of "FITness" (fluency in information technology, now called "ICT fluency"), the challenge has been in trying to institutionalize those kinds of outcomes within the schools' practices and curricula, even its institutional culture.

Repeated calls from the corporate and higher-education communities for high school graduates to come to the workplace or postsecondary institutions as problem-solvers, adaptive and self-motivated learners, collaborators, and critical thinkers have not been enough (AeA, 2005; Partnership for the 21st Century, 2004). Planning committee member Dan Gohl has a vision of our schools looking more like the workplaces of the 21st century than the schools of the 20th century, but the transformative institutional efforts to move us closer to that goal have been, at best, disappointing. Workshop participants attributed the lack of progress both to inherent obstacles in the institution of K–12 schooling and the lack of agreement about what aspects of ICT fluency the schools should be responsible for fostering in the first place.

Being Fluent articulates, through its FITness framework, an important continuum of skills, concepts, and intellectual capabilities. ICT is not only a "thing" like an integrated circuit or the World Wide Web; it is also an application of hardware and software in the service of cognitive and professional growth. The result is a revolutionary new space for knowledge-generation and its digital representation (Horwitz, see Appendix B). It is a space that can link a wide community of learners and thinkers, where our capacities can advance through the intersection of people's social and individual inclinations.

John Seely Brown (2002, p. 6) describes this very real phenomenon as follows:

> It's interesting to watch how new systems get absorbed by society; with the Web, this absorption, or learning process, by young people has been quite different from the process in times past. My generation tends not to want to try things unless or until we already know how to use them. If we don't know how to use some appliance or software, our instinct is to reach for a manual or take a course or call up an expert. Believe me, hand a manual or suggest a course to 15 year olds and they think you are a dinosaur. They want to turn the thing on, get in there, muck around, see what works. Today's kids get on the Web and link, lurk, and watch how other people are doing things, then try it themselves. . . . Learning becomes situated in action; it becomes as much social as cognitive, it is concrete rather than abstract.

Yet as Bell points out (see Appendix C), the existing FITness framework described in *Being Fluent* is predominantly based on an individual construct of ICT fluency. It notes, for example, that "FITness is a body of knowledge and understanding that enables individuals to use information technology effectively in a variety of different contexts" (National Research Council 1999, p. 40). But Bell, like Brown, suggests that expertise and ultimate solutions mediated through ICT are often to be found in distributed groups or communities and not just in the mind of the individual. "Generally, individuals routinely leverage their social networks to identify useful knowledge and relevant learning resources as part of their day-to-day dealings," Bell writes. "For those immersed within what could be characterized as an ICT learning community, they may learn about new technological systems and approaches from others in their social network."

Vera Michalchik emphasizes the social and cultural dimensions associated with information and communication technology, stressing how difficult it is to separate the technology from the social context of the user (V.

Michalchik, personal communication, ICT Workshop on October 26, 2005, Washington, DC.). Results of ethnographic studies reveal that ICT is adopted and adapted differently, depending on one's social situation and the ways in which the technology will be used. Moreover, ICT creates new social spaces as people learn about, negotiate, communicate with, and apply new technologies, thereby connecting with each other in interdependent and generative ways that are deeply social in their own right.

Thus, both Bell and Michalchik appear to be calling up a picture of interdependent learning as a core feature of information and communication technology. But this image stands in contrast to the existing culture of formal schooling, which is based on a system of individual accomplishment. This contrast raises questions about the degree to which, or whether, the inherently complex, pervasive, and social ICT can fit into the present K–12 system.

Future inquiries into how information and communication technology can become successfully established in formal learning institutions would do well to first explore how high-school-aged youth are engaging with ICT outside school and then to determine the implications for such learning processes *inside* school. As workshop participants noted, the social dimensions of learning and applying ICT are a critical and frequently overlooked dimension of understanding how ICT fits in high schools or in K–12 schools in general. In particular, we need to understand more fully what kinds of ICT skills, competencies, and capabilities high school students are now acquiring in their daily, informal, and highly social uses of ICT and whether these pursuits give them fluency as defined in *Being Fluent*. Only then can we chart a path toward high schools that advance students' ICT fluency at the same time as they enrich them with knowledge and skills in literature, history, mathematics, science, and other core subjects.

REFERENCES

AeA. (2005). *Losing the competitive advantage? The challenge for science and technology in the United States.* Available: http://www.aeanet.org/publications/IDJJ_AeA_ Competitiveness.asp [accessed March 1, 2006].

Brown, J.S. (2002). Growing up digital: How the web changes work, education, and the ways people learn. *USDLA Journal, 16*(2). Available: http:///www.usdla.org/html/ journalFEB02_Issues/article01.html. [March 1, 2006].

National Research Council. (1999). *Being fluent with information technology.* Washington, DC.: National Academy Press.

Partnership for the 21st Century. (2004). *Learning for the 21st century.* Available: http:// www.21stcenturyskills.org/downloads/P21_Report.pdf. [accessed March 1, 2006].

Appendix A

ICT Fluency: Content and Context

Karen Pittman

My observations begin with the content of the components of fluency framework (see Box 2-1) but move fairly quickly to thoughts about the contexts in which young people can and should be encouraged to learn, practice, and apply this content. From where I sit, the components of fluency framework does include the menu of skills, concepts, and capabilities that are important and that have—in many cases—been included in other frameworks. More important than the specific items, however, the framework as a whole acknowledges the three important layers of learning that are needed in order to be "fluent" in the 21st century. But there is a challenge.

As presented on the page, it is not clear that the three lists of indicators represent different levels of fluency. All indicators appear equal. But they are not. The skills indicators are narrower and much more specific to information and communications technology (ICT) fluency than the others. And many people would argue that mastery of many of the intellectual capabilities is neither dependent on having ICT skills nor in the sole domain of ICT fluency.

The specific skills, concepts, and capabilities listed differ in scope and importance, and the underlying assumptions about how students develop skills, concepts, and capabilities are also different. The assumptions about how ICT skills, concepts, and capabilities relate to one another should, therefore, be made much more explicit. It should be obvious at a glance that no one is trying to equate building a spreadsheet with sustained reasoning. Any of a number of graphic tricks would make this clear (e.g., linking skills to concepts to capabilities with arrows that lead upward or putting the lists in nested boxes.) The layering used by the Partnership for 21st Century Skills (2003), for example (core subjects, learning skills, 21st century context, 21st century content, etc.), has proven effective.

Having offered comments on the content of the framework, let me move on quickly to context. The skills list is certainly the narrowest of the three areas, but it may be the most important from a student engagement perspective. This is an area where students—even students lacking in some of the basic concepts and capabilities—increasingly bring prior knowledge and experience to the table, with technology becoming so prevalent in their personal lives. (When a nationally representative sample of 10- to 17-year-olds were recently asked what skills they need more experience with in order to be successful in life, technology skills actually ranked close to the bottom—after financial, job, life, communication, people, thinking, academic, and cultural skills [America's Promise, 2005]).

From an implementation perspective, it is reasonable to argue that young people who have the intellectual capabilities identified in the framework will have an easier time acquiring specific concepts and technology skills. The power of the argument for ICT fluency, however, may lie in the fact that the more effective engagement strategy may actually be to work up from the bottom, with specific skills as a starting point.

The arguments become much more persuasive when the framework is presented as an answer to a bigger question: How can we capitalize on the fact that youths increasingly have and want to use skills, in order to teach the concepts underlying those skills and then push further to the build the larger intellectual capabilities?

Coming in the skills door also helps illustrate how and why schools are critical but not the only important setting that must be part of the conversation. I think we can all agree that the worst thing we could do is turn a natural skill acquisition space into a rote technology class or static curriculum. We must figure out how to integrate the application of technology skills plus the development of new skills into engaging learning contexts in which the development of the underlying concepts and intellectual capabilities are embedded learning goals.

People learn these skills and concepts through project-based, applied learning opportunities, as discussed in *Being Fluent* (National Research Council, 1999) Applied learning happens in school buildings and in the broader community, both during the school day and beyond. In fact, we would be in deep trouble if there weren't applied learning opportunities all over the place, since not every young person we are trying to reach can be found in school. Knowing that roughly one-third of all teens (and nearly one-half of all teens of color) do not graduate from high school makes it all the more critical that opportunities to learn and apply technology and other skills be available in school and out.

The question isn't whether learning opportunities outside of the traditional classroom and school day are important. The question is why these opportunities are considered beyond or even peripheral to mainstream conversations about learning and high school reform. Research by Reed Larson (2000) and his colleagues suggest that American adolescents spend only a small fraction of their days fully engaged—meaning in contexts where they consistently report high challenge, high concentration, and high motivation. More often than not, the daily context for this high engagement is not school, but structured, voluntary activities such as internships, extracurricular clubs, community service projects, and youth programs.

School must be at the center of the solution. But the nonschool hours represent too significant an opportunity to be left out of the conversation. And nonschool partners—families, community-based youth organizations, businesses, libraries, faith communities, and cultural institutions—represent too significant an asset to be left cheering on the sidelines.

For example, in Seattle, Washington, low-income teens are employed as technology experts at King County branch libraries, providing computer assistance to library patrons. In San Diego, students in afterschool multimedia arts and civic engagement program work on new media journalism, digital photography, and graphic design projects while acquiring basic journalism skills. In Santa Cruz, middle school girls spend time at their local Boys and Girls Club during the summer creating computer games with interactive story narratives using Micromedia's Flash program. And every year at the Education Video Center, in New York City, 60 high school students learn to write, shoot, and edit documentaries on issues that impact their lives as urban teens, learning media analysis and video documentary production on state-of-the-art equipment during a semester-long workshop for which they earn high school credit.

I am not trying to suggest that community programs are a silver bullet or that we should shut down high schools and let students join youth programs. The point is that high-yield learning environments can be found or created in school and out. If the broad goal of the K–12 system is to ensure students leave school ready for the future, the changes that are necessary can be complemented by—and perhaps only fully implemented through—intentional collaboration with community partners. The vision of community education partnerships put forth by Paul Hill and colleagues (2000) in *It Takes a City* helps articulate this goal, by recognizing that "the traditional boundaries between the public school system's responsibilities and those of other community agencies are themselves a part of the educational problem."

REFERENCES

America's Promise. (2005). *Voices study research findings.* Alexandria, VA: Author. Available: http://www.americaspromise.org/files/AP%20VOICES%20STUDY.pdf. (Accessed June 2006].

Hill, P.T., Campbell, C., and Harvey, J. (2000). *It takes a city: Getting serious about urban school reform.* Washington, DC: Brookings Institution Press.

Larson, R. (2000). Toward a psychology of positive youth development. *American Psychologist, 55*(1), 170–183.

National Research Council. (1999). *Being fluent with information technology.* Committee on Information Technology Literacy. Washington, DC: National Academy Press.

Partnership for 21st Century Skills. (2003). *Learning for the 21st century: A report and MILE guide for 21st century skills.* Washington, DC: Author.

Appendix B

Achieving Information and Communications Technology (ICT) Fluency: Is Nothing New Under the Sun?

Paul Horwitz

Imagine that the year is 1500. The printing press is 50 years old, about as old as the computer is today. Cheap, printed books, mostly from Venice, are beginning to flow across Europe. As a result, new demands are being placed on education: Suddenly, it has become important for ordinary people, not just those who will enter the clergy or study law, to be able to read. And reading, it is becoming clear, in contrast to other useful skills like blacksmithing or shoemaking, cannot be learned by apprenticeship—it requires a special kind of place called a "school." So formal education is becoming a requirement for a growing middle class.[1]

Will the computer have the same kind of far-reaching effect on education that the printing press had 500 years ago? Are there things that students today need to know that they don't learn in the traditional school environment? If so, what are those things, and what should we be doing to ensure that they are taught and learned?

Superficially, one can imagine that computers raise no educational issues not covered already by books and other media. After all, we already teach our children how to read. What difference can it possibly make

---

[1] For an in-depth look at the societal effects of the printing press, including its effects on education, see (1979). E. Eisenstein, *The printing press as an agent of change.* Cambridge, England: Cambridge University Press.

whether the words are on a horizontal surface or a vertical one? And as for so-called "multimedia," movies have been around for over a century and still pictures since the caveman. Do we really care what kind of screen we view them on?

But it's not that simple. The computer is not a book, neither is it a library, an art gallery, or a movie theater. And reading on a computer is fundamentally different from reading a book, or a newspaper, or a scholarly article. On a computer, text tends to come in small snippets (for a reason that is still unclear, no one wants to read much more than one screen at a time) connected to each other by hyperlinks created by the author. Sometimes the semantics behind those links is obvious, sometimes it is obscure—and sometimes the link leads to a different Website altogether, which may have been created for a slightly different purpose and audience. To "read" a computer, students need to learn how to follow hypertext links without getting lost or forgetting what their original intent was; they need to master a certain form of nonlinear thinking.

The plethora of unfiltered information available on the Web also places increased emphasis on students' ability to evaluate that information, to identify disinformation and propaganda, and to check sources for consistency and coherence. In one of the more useful neologisms of this age of the search engine, our students need to learn how to Google. This knowledge involves much more than typing a key word or phrase and then browsing the first 10,000th of 1 percent of the resulting hits. Students must learn how to make sense of all that information, how to place it in context, connect it with their existing knowledge, and run it past an internal censor before accepting it.

There is an interesting parallel between the invention of printing and the appearance of the modern search engine. Even as printed books increased the importance of reading, they were devaluing another, more ancient, skill: that of memorization. Today, we find it remarkable that before the 16th century so many educated people were able to memorize the Bible or the complete works of Cicero. The "literature" of authors such as Homer depended on such prodigious feats of memory, the art of which has now been abandoned in favor of techniques for rapidly locating information in books. By automating the search process and making it vastly more powerful, Google is making such "librarian skills" obsolete while simultaneously raising concerns about what new knowledge students will need if they are to manage their new-found powers wisely.

WHY SHOULD ICT FLUENCY
BE RESTRICTED TO LANGUAGE?

Powerful though those applications are, to consider the computer as nothing more than a replacement for books and other media is to vastly underestimate its potential effect on education. Computers can do much more than communicate, whether in text or multimedia. They are tools that can do many things, and to be information and communications technology (ICT) fluent should entail knowing what those things are, being able to get computers to do them, and understanding their utility, their potential misuses, and their limitations. I offer two examples.

Computers can implement and run numerical models of naturally occurring phenomena, and indeed their use in this capacity has revolutionized many areas of science, mathematics, and engineering. Accordingly, whether or not they intend to enter these fields, 21st century students should know something about how computers are used for modeling everything from global climate change to the behavior of airfoils. They do not need to know how to build such models, or even how to use them, but they should know that they exist, how they are used, and what their limitations are.

Computers are routinely used to store and provide access to a great deal of personal information about individuals. Often this information is collected in quite informal ways: for example, personal networking Websites like Friendsters (http://www.friendster.com) generally request that new members fill out questionnaires. Although this action is entirely voluntary, and notwithstanding the posting of explicit privacy policies by the Websites, students are often unaware of the potentially damaging consequences of posting personal information on the Web where it may remain accessible for a very long time. ICT fluency should include awareness of the potential dangers of the misuse of databases.

SHOULD KIDS BECOME ICT FLUENT IN SCHOOL?

Although the workshop and the report that will emerge from it are primarily interested in the role that formal and informal educational institutions can play in helping youngsters become fluent in ICT, it is important to recognize that the process is going on apace every day, largely outside those adult-ridden environments. The rise of massive multiplayer on-line role-playing games (MMORPGs)—Everquest claimed more than

375,000 active players in 2003, World of Warcraft probably has many more—is a social phenomenon of immense proportions and unpredictable potential, affecting young people disproportionately (the mean age of Starcraft players is 18.3).[2]

Cellphones are rapidly becoming computers (or is it the other way around?) that kids learn about and, for the most part, use outside the classroom. Should ICT fluency encompass these and other emerging technologies? If so, should fluency with them be the subject of school-based curricula? Though I would answer "yes" to the first question, my tendency is to say "no" to the second in most cases. Every sufficiently powerful new technology brings new challenges and opportunities; that doesn't mean that every such technology should be taught in school. The automobile, for instance, is certainly a powerful, ubiquitous, and potentially dangerous technology, yet although driver's education courses are taught in many schools, they are hardly considered part of the core curriculum. They are offered on the school premises as a convenience, not because mastery of the automobile is seen as an important goal of education. If kids become fluent in ICT largely outside of school, that is probably a desirable, as much as inevitable, outcome.

Yet, as I touched on above, I have a feeling (though I have no statistics to back up this up) that people—youngsters and adults alike—have a tendency to trust computers much too much and then to be unduly critical when a technological model leads them astray. A weather model is not, and never can be, 100 percent accurate; yet weather predictions based on computer models are more reliable than horoscopes (which may well be generated by computers, for all I know). To the extent that an ever-increasing percentage of what we believe to be true is based on computer models, people need to be sophisticated in their assessments of the value and reliability of those beliefs. To instill that sophistication should be a primary goal of 21st century schools.

---

[2]Available: http://www.nickyee.com/eqt/demographics.html.

Appendix C

Cognitive and Social Foundations of Information and Communications Technology (ICT) Fluency

Philip Bell

Since the publication of the *Being Fluent with Information Technology* report (National Research Council,1999), the importance of the topic has only increased in societal importance—even with the dramatic decline and reconstitution of the associated ICT industries. K–12 schools have continued efforts to expand access to ICT, provide the necessary computer network infrastructure, and engage teachers in relevant professional development and curricular integration activities. Also, research focused on exploring the unique affordances of ICT in formal education settings still seems to be on the rise, as evidenced, in part, by the concentrated focus on ICT in the learning sciences community in terms of research activities and scholarship. And importantly, specific ICTs have become cornerstones of the everyday activities and culture of youth—ICTs have become fully integrated into the texture of their routine daily activities (e.g., Ito, 2004; Lenhart, Rainie and Lewis, 2001).

In this paper I briefly consider two facets of a contemporary understanding of information technology fluency. First, I consider the existing FITness framework from the perspective of the research literature on cognition and learning. Second, I develop what might be considered a new framework dimension consisting of *FIT social practices* that enable, contribute to, or in some cases fully constitute ICT fluencies in the 21st century.

There seems to be a tension in the *Being Fluent* report (National Research Council, 1999) related to how FITness was bounded. This tension can perhaps be summarized by two framing questions:

1. What aspects of computer science should citizens understand with regard to ICTs?
2. What understanding of and competencies with ICTs should citizens possess?

Although some people may see these as equivalent questions, I take them to be overlapping and somewhat divergent ways of being fluent. I take the second one as being more inclusive of a range of sophisticated everyday activities associated with ICT that do not necessarily connect to an understanding of computer science (e.g., being able to participate in a variety of ICT modes of communication, using ICT to inform personal decisions). In this paper, I consider both frames on FITness to be important, given the set of rationales enumerated in the report and ICT trends in society.[1]

THE COGNITIVE AND LEARNING FOUNDATIONS OF FITNESS

The *Being Fluent* report presents a tripartite FITness framework consisting of intellectual capabilities, concepts, and skills associated with ICT fluency. To date, the cognitive and learning sciences have only focused on specific segments of the ICT domain. In order to explore select aspects of the cognitive and learning foundations of the FITness framework, I begin by asserting some connections to general principles or characteristics of cognition and learning and then describe some areas of specific research on FITness components. It should be noted that having to rely on general principles is less than ideal; below I also detail a research agenda that would help advance the field.

Problem Solving As one might expect, there are many connections to be made between accounts of problem solving and many of the components of FITness—from principled and disciplinary identification and specification of a problem (see Box 2-1, intellectual capabilities #1), to the decomposition of problems and the sequencing of corresponding components of a problem solution (intellectual capabilities #2), and to the broader utility of more abstract domain knowledge (intellectual capabilities #10). It

---

[1]I do see evidence of both fluency frames in the 1999 report, although there is more of the first than of the second. Perhaps it was a natural result of working within the constraints of the 30 components of FITness.

is worth noting that beyond the relevance of these general features of problem solving associated with ICT fluency, many features of ICT expertise involve domain-specific problem solving. For example, the details of quality debugging procedures while programming (cf. intellectual capabilities #4) are best understood through direct empirical studies of programmers rather than relying on general principles.

Metacognition, Learning, and Trouble Shooting A broad range of research has highlighted the benefits of metacognition when learning—about concepts and inquiry—and when engaging in problem solving (National Research Council, 2000, for a summary of much of this research). Similar benefits of reflection are referenced in that report with regard to the cultivation of more abstract knowledge about technology. Beyond this one explicit reference, there is likely an important role to be played by metacognition associated with the intellectual capabilities associated with "testing a solution" (see intellectual capabilities #3) and "managing problems in faulty solutions" (intellectual capabilities #4) (e.g., during fault identification as part of troubleshooting; Frederiksen and White, 1998) as well as with the cultivation of technological concepts (cf. the conceptual change in science research of White and Frederiksen, 1998).

It is also useful to note the central importance of using a mental model for the system in question during associated reasoning processes. Frederiksen and White (1998) argue for the benefits of functional models in particular, which reveal the device-centered propagation of system effects, to aid in troubleshooting complex technical systems.

Organizing, Navigating, and Evaluating Information There is extensive literature on how people process and manage information, and the 1999 report gives a fair amount of attention to the matter (see intellectual capabilities #5 and the section on "information literacy"). Since the publication of the report, learning scientists have continued to document how ICTs can be used in educational settings to support students in disciplinary learning and inquiry. For example, Web-based Inquiry Science Environment (WISE) Project has explored how to support students in important epistemic practices associated with the natural sciences (e.g., forms of scientific argumentation, critique, and design) as they critically engage with scientific information from the Web (Bell and Linn, 2000; see Linn, Davis and Bell, 2004, for a summary of a decade of such research). This project is similar in kind to the Kids as Global Scientists effort discussed in the NRC report.

More generally, there are a range of similarly motivated research projects that have explored such things as scaffolding students' explanation of complex scientific data sets (Edelson, Gordin, and Pea, 1999; Sandoval and Reiser, 2004) and engaging students in scientific modeling linked to complex data sets over the network (Horowitz, 1996). One aspect of these efforts that sets them apart from "information literacy" approaches to information evaluation has to do with the discipline-specific focus of how students are supported in working with the information at hand—the epistemological criteria used for information and data, the nature of the "theory work" at hand, and the underlying conceptual details that are implicated in the analysis. In other words, one would not want to have students interpret a piece of historical information in the same way as information derived from a scientific experiment (see Stevens, Wineburg, Herrenkohl, and Bell, 2005, for a relevant description of a research agenda associated with developing a comparative understanding of school subjects).

FIT Research Priorities My own sense is that there are significant gaps in the FITness literature, especially when one takes a more "whole cloth" approach to understanding the associated learning phenomena— across cognitive, affective, social, and cultural dimensions. This is particularly the case in the context of rapidly evolving technologies. Let me briefly detail one example to highlight this kind of gap. Consider the proliferation of chat and instant messaging technologies in youth cultures over the past 5 years—involving synchronous, multistranded textual exchanges among groups.[2] Such exchanges involve arguably new forms of social interaction mediated by specific technological implementations (e.g., intermixed strands of discourse from a variety of participants who may or may not know each other), as well as significant linguistic stylization (see Crystal, 2001).

An understanding of the cognitive and learning phenomena at play within such technological environments might consider dimensions of text comprehension, working memory, specialized linguistic registers, novel interactional processes, and related microcultural processes (e.g., establishing participation norms). And, frequently, youth are engaged in chat or IM (instant messaging) activities while "time cycling" with one or more other

---

[2]The National Research Council report makes reference to chat communication technologies, but it is not a central feature of the existing FITness framework relative to its prevalence among youth in the workforce.

activities or parallel communication sessions. It should also be noted that workers are also frequently instant messaging with collaborators these days as constituent parts of larger, collective work efforts. Some of the foundational research of the kind I am describing exists for chat and instant messaging (e.g., Schönfeldt and Golato, 2003), but much remains to be done—especially with appropriate attention given to FITness.

With this kind of "whole cloth" orientation, let me discuss a couple of research directions that need to be pursued more systematically. First, many youth communities are vigorously adopting and customizing ICTs for their own purposes (e.g., social networking, multimedia journaling, entertainment). These uses in many cases represent sophisticated and authentic ICT fluency, and we need to directly observe and systematically understand how such activities are accomplished in the naturalistic settings where they occur.. This everyday cognition ICT agenda would allow us to do the following: (a) confirm the ecological validity of specific FITness components; (b) investigate how FITness components are coordinated in action and more generally interrelated; (c) potentially identify important, "missing" components of ICT fluency associated with contemporary fluency with a range of quickly evolving technologies (e.g., blogs, wiki, IM, gaming engines, podcasting); and project domains (e.g., civic engagement, open source development, family communication), and (d) document the learning ecologies associated with sophisticated ICT fluency (see Barron, 2004).

A second research priority naturally follows from the products of the first. After documenting the range of ICT fluencies associated with a specific population (e.g., high school students) for a particular kind of project, educational research could then be mounted to learn how to bring such fluencies to broader populations. This sequencing of research should serve to enhance the ecological grounding of educational ICT efforts. A related kind of ecological grounding might also be accomplished by systematically observing students learning about FITness in their projects that take place outside of the bounds of the original course.[3]

A third research agenda—already enumerated above—might focus on developing a comparative understanding of how ICTs can support

---

[3] Versions of the first two of these research priorities are currently being pursued in the learning in informal and formal environments (LIFE) science of learning center funded by the National Science Foundation: for more details on this effort see http://life-slc.org/ as well as Bransford et al. (in press).

disciplinary-specific learning and accomplishment (e.g., how it can support a student in thinking more like a mathematician versus thinking more like a scientist).

FIT SOCIAL PRACTICES

The existing FITness framework is predominantly framed around an individual-mentalistic construct of ICT fluency—as evidenced by this quote from the *Being Fluent* report, (National Research Council, 1999):

> FITness is a body of knowledge and understanding that enables individuals to use information technology effectively in a variety of different contexts. (p. 40)

I believe it is fruitful to leverage the "practice turn" associated with recent research on human learning and development (see Jessor, 1996; Schatzki, Knorr Cetina, and von Savigny, 2001) in order to consider social practices that seem to be important components of FITness. In this section I highlight two candidate social practices documented in sociocultural research on sophisticated ICT use. Taken together, these components can be used to argue for a new framework dimension consisting of FIT social practices that enable, contribute to, or in some cases fully constitute ICT fluencies.

Cultivating and Participating in a FIT Learning Community Governed by Shared Norms Associated with Distributed Expertise Solutions to ICT problems sometimes reside in distributed communities—not in the mind of an individual who encounters a given problem. It is an important form of ICT fluency to be able to locate or broker a solution from individuals in such a community. Generally, individuals routinely leverage their social networks to identify useful knowledge and relevant learning resources as part of their day-to-day dealings. For those immersed in what could be characterized as an ICT learning community,[4] they may learn about new technological systems and approaches from others in their social network. They consult individuals with different kinds of expertise to aid in solving problems being encountered. Networked forums and other forms of electronic communication allow for these ICT learning communities to be geographically distributed and inclusive of diverse forms of expertise. Simi-

---

[4]An ICT learning community can be considered a specialized form of what Engelbart has referred to as a "networked improvement community."

larly, Barron's research on the development of technological fluencies has identified how individuals navigate their "learning ecologies" to best effect during their technology design and development work—which includes tapping others with different knowledge (Barron, 2004).

In our ethnographic research on the technological fluencies of undergraduate engineers (Bell and Zimmerman, 2005), we have documented an interesting social norm associated with an ICT learning communities. These undergraduates have established sets of blogs to share various kinds of information about their technological activities. Through our observations and interviews it has become apparent that this distributed, informal learning community maintains its vibrancy—its growing information database and hence its utility—through a shared social expectation of individuals systematically contributing newly acquired information to the community through their personal blogs as a routine course of daily affairs (i.e., before anyone expresses a need for that particular information). By routinely documenting their problems and associated solutions in these on-line information spaces, the community is facilitating the future ICT problem solving of others and making the distributed expertise of the group more readily available.

I am arguing that being able to participate in these kinds of informal learning communities—where distributed expertise is the norm and collective practices are in place to share expertise and "hard won" practical knowledge—is an important, and perhaps even a foundational, form of ICT fluency. I fully expect to find similarly constituted ICT learning communities in the workplace as well as in education.

Storytelling as a Means of Bridging the Abstract to the Concrete and Vice Versa Occupational communities make central use of storytelling in order to function. In his ethnographic research studying the social and technical activities of photocopier technicians, Orr (1996) documented how the routine production and exchange of technology-related narratives serve to (a) describe the "ill structured" problems encountered in the field: (b) convey relevant information and past solutions among technicians, customers, and management; (c) situate information for use in a given context (i.e., to bridge from the abstract to the concrete); and (d) diagnose issues in order to make problems soluble.[5]

---

[5]Other social functions of narratives, further afield from FITness, include demonstrating competence to colleagues and customers, maintaining social bonds among clients and technicians, demonstrating organizational hierarchy, and group memberships and defining boundaries (see Orr, 1996, for details).

The nature of human development prepares people to engage in sophisticated forms of narrative cognition and communication (Bruner, 1987). Being able to engage in ICT storytelling—to construct and interpret narratives that map onto problems and projects—can then be thought of as a foundational practice associated with information technology fluency. Interpreted from the perspective of this social practice, sustained reasoning (see intellectual capability #1) is often a social process.

Educational Implications of FIT Social Practices I believe the two aforementioned social practices serve to exemplify a possible way to elaborate the FITness framework. They also provide insight into ICT education. As is more generally the case, social practices provide relatively concrete images of how students can be engaged in activity as part of educational experiences. In this case, students learning about information technology could be systematically brought into the two sets of practices outlined above. First, they could form (or join) an ICT learning community and learn the social norms associated with operating as a distributed expertise community. Second, through appropriate modeling and scaffolding, students could learn how to engage in productive ICT storytelling related to their own projects and problems. In the process, students would likely be learning relevant intellectual capabilities, fundamental concepts, and contemporary skills. It is possible that through team-based courses, many students likely are being brought into such practices—but I believe it would be helpful to more explicitly focus on these social practices as fluency outcomes to be cultivated through educational efforts.

REFERENCES

Barron, B. (2004). Learning ecologies for technological fluency: Gender and experience differences. *Journal Educational Computing Research, 31*(1), 1–36.

Bell, P., and Linn, M.C. (2000). Scientific arguments as learning artifacts: Designing for learning from the web with KIE. *International Journal of Science Education, 22*(8), 797–817.

Bell, P., and Zimmerman, H.T. (2005). *The informal learning processes of expert technologists learning about technology.* Unpublished paper, University of Washington, Seattle.

Bransford, J., Vye, N., Stevens, R., Kuhl, P., Schwartz, D., Bell, P., Meltzoff, A., Barron, B., Pea, R., Reeves, B., Roschelle, J., and Sabelli, N. (in press). Learning theories and education: Toward a decade of synergy. In P. Alexander and P. Winne (Eds.), *Handbook of educational psychology* (Second Edition). Mahwah, NJ: Erlbaum.

Bruner, J. (1987). Two modes of thought. In *Actual minds, possible worlds* (pp. 11-43). Cambridge, MA: Harvard University Press.

Crystal, D. (2001). *Language and the Internet.* Cambridge, England: Cambridge University Press.

Edelson, D.C., Gordin, D.N., and Pea, R.D. (1999). Addressing the challenges of inquiry-based learning through technology and curriculum design. *Journal of the Learning Sciences, 8*(3-4), 391–450.

Frederiksen, J., and White, B. (1998). Teaching and learning generic modeling and reasoning skills. *Journal of Interactive Learning Environments, 5,* 33–51.

Horwitz, P. (1996). Linking models to data: Hypermodels for science education. *The High School Journal, 79*(2), 148–156.

Ito, M. (2004). *Personal portable pedestrian: Lessons from Japanese mobile phone use.* Paper presented at the Mobile Communication and Social Change: The 2004 International Conference on Mobile Communication, Seoul, Korea.

Jessor, R. (1996). Ethnographic methods in contemporary perspective. In R. Jessor, A. Colby, and R.A. Shweder (Eds.), *Ethnography and human development* (pp. 3–14). Chicago: University of Chicago Press.

Lenhart, A., Rainie, L., and Lewis, O. (2001). *Teenage life online: The rise of the instant-message generation and the Internet's impact on friendships and family relationships.* Washington, DC: Pew Internet and American Life Project.

Linn, M.C., Davis, E.A., and Bell, P. (2004). *Internet environments for science education.* Mahwah, NJ: Erlbaum.

National Research Council. (1999). *Being fluent with information technology.* Committee on Information Technology Literacy. Washington, DC: National Academy Press.

National Research Council. (2000). *How people learn: Brain, mind, experience, and school.* J.D. Bransford, A.L. Brown, and R.R. Cocking (Eds.). Committee on Developments in the Science of Learning with additional material from the Committee on Learning Research and Educational Practice. Washington, DC: National Academy Press.

Orr, J.E. (1996). *Talking about machines: An ethnography of a modern job.* Ithaca, NY: ILR Press.

Sandoval, W.A., and Reiser, B.J. (2004). Explanation-driven inquiry: Integrating conceptual and epistemic scaffolds for scientific inquiry. *Science Education, 88,* 345–372.

Schatzki, T., Knorr Cetina, K., and von Savigny, E. (Eds.). (2001). *The practice turn in contemporary theory.* London, England: Routledge.

Schönfeldt, J., and Golato, A. (2003). Repair in chats: A conversation analytic approach. *Research on Language and Social Interaction, 36*(3), 241–284.

Stevens, R., Wineburg, S., Herrenkohl, L. R., and Bell, P. (2005). The comparative understanding of school subjects: Past, present, and future research agenda. *Review of Educational Research, 75*(2), 125–157.

White, B.Y., and Frederiksen, J.R. (1998). Inquiry, modeling, and metacognition: Making science accessible to all students. *Cognition and Instruction, 16*(1), 3–118.

Appendix D
Information and Communications Technology (ICT) Fluency: What Do All High School Students Need to Know?

Paul Resta

ICT ELEMENTS

I believe the elements of the ICT fluency framework are still relevant and appropriate. It will be important, however, to compare the elements against other elements that have been developed. The Partnership for 21st Century Skills (2003) identified a number of skills that should be considered in a review of the initial framework for ICT literacy. These include: self-direction, interpersonal skills, accountability and adaptability, and social responsibility. The Educational Testing Service (ETS) has also developed a new assessment for ICT literacy. It has defined the following seven proficiencies for ICT literacy (Educational Testing Service, 2005).

Access: The ability to collect and/or retrieve information in digital environments. This includes the ability to identify likely digital information sources and to get the information from these sources.

Manage: The ability to apply an existing organizational or classification scheme for digital information. This ability focuses on reorganizing existing digital information from a single source using pre-existing organizational formats. It includes the ability to identify pre-existing organization schemes, select appropriate schemes for the current usage, and apply the schemes.

Integrate: The ability to interpret and represent digital information. This includes the ability to use ICT tools to synthesize, summarize, and compare information from multiple digital sources.

Evaluate: The ability to determine the degree to which digital information satisfies the needs of the task in ICT environments. This includes the ability to judge the quality, relevance, authority, point of view/bias, currency, coverage, or accuracy of digital information.

Create: The ability to generate information by adapting, applying, designing, or inventing information in ICT environments.

Communicate: The ability to communicate information properly in its context of use for ICT environments. This includes the ability to gear electronic information for a particular audience and to communicate knowledge in the appropriate venue.

I think it is important to review the 21st Century Skills and ETS ICT literacy elements to determine if new elements should be added to the fluency framework.

ASSESSMENT OF FLUENCY

In addition to the assessment instrument developed by ETS, it will be important to consider the use of more authentic and performance-based measures to diagnose and assess the extent to which a student has mastered and integrated the three aspects of fluency: intellectual capabilities, concepts, and skills. Such an approach may require the use of multiple forms of evidence, including student products and performances. Such an approach should not represent an "add-on" to the present assessment process, but rather a rethinking of the assessment process to more tightly couple core content knowledge with ICT fluency.

PEDAGOGICAL PRACTICES

We should also discuss perhaps the greatest challenge to achieving ICT fluency, changing pedagogical practices. Implementation Considerations, Chapter 4 in *Being Fluent*, advocates a project-based approach to developing FITness and recognizes that lecturing about fluency is not an optimal form of instruction. This idea needs expansion to more fully develop the pedagogical implications of helping students achieve ICT fluency. It should offer recommendations and strategies to teacher education institutions to help them prepare a new generation of teachers who are able to foster ICT fluency in their students.

The importance of providing blended learning environments—face-to-face and online— should be discussed as an important element in helping students become fluent. Electronic collaboration is changing the ways that work is accomplished, and electronic proximity increasingly represents the new workspace. Schools need to provide opportunities for students to work effectively in both the classroom and online environments.

CONTEXTS

Fluency is best developed when students are engaged in authentic tasks, in authentic contexts, using authentic 21st century tools. Apprenticeships, internships, and service learning programs enable students to apply their academic and ICT skills in real-world settings. Such programs require developing more flexible scheduling and close collaboration with local businesses, industries, medical facilities, engineering firms, and other organizations. Providing such opportunities will enhance the ICT skills of all students, but they will be particularly important for minority students, individuals with disabilities, and students from economically disadvantaged families.

Service learning may also be used to help students develop fluency as they engage in meaningful service to their schools and communities. In this context, students apply their academic and ICT skills to solve real-world issues and problems, working with adults as partners in the process.

I offer examples of such programs:

- the GenY Program, in which students assist teachers in technology use and support the technology functions of the school (Arizona Learning Interchange, 2005); and
- the Microsoft High School Intern Program, in which students are exposed to technology and encouraged to pursue high-tech professions (Microsoft, 2005).

Such efforts will go far toward strengthening the connection between schools and workplaces and will enable students to develop a deeper level of understanding of the importance and ubiquity of technology in the work place.

REFERENCES

Arizona Learning Interchange. (2005). *GenY: "Y" students are with teacher to change education.* Available: http://ali.apple.com/ali_sites/azli/exhibits/1000609/ Resources.html. [accessed October 27, 2005].

Educational Testing Service. (2005). *ETS ICT literacy assessment.* Available: http:www.ets.org. [accessed September 27, 2005].

Microsoft. (2005). *Microsoft high school intern program.* Available: http://www.microsoft.com/ College/highschool/highschool.mspx. [accessed September 27, 2005].

Partnership for 21st Century Skills. (2003*). Learning for the 21st century: A report and MILE guide for 21st century skills.* Tucson, AZ: Author.